Books are to be returned on or before
the last date

4 MAY 2001

OCT 2001

The JOURNEYS of ST. PAUL

THE LIVING BIBLE

The JOURNEYS *of* ST. PAUL

JAMES HARPUR

REV. MARCUS BRAYBROOKE
CONSULTANT

MARSHALL PUBLISHING • LONDON

A MARSHALL EDITION
Conceived, edited and designed by
MARSHALL EDITIONS LTD
170 Piccadilly, London W1V 9DD

First published in the UK in 1997 by Marshall Publishing Ltd

PROJECT EDITOR: THERESA LANE
PROJECT ART EDITOR: HELEN SPENCER
PICTURE EDITOR: ELIZABETH LOVING
RESEARCH: JAMES RANKIN
COPY EDITOR: JOLIKA FESZT
INDEXER: JUDY BATCHELOR
MANAGING EDITOR: LINDSAY MCTEAGUE
PRODUCTION EDITOR: EMMA DIXON
PRODUCTION: NIKKI INGRAM
ART DIRECTOR: SEAN KEOGH
EDITORIAL DIRECTOR: SOPHIE COLLINS

The publishers acknowledge Rev. Marcus Braybrooke as author
of the "Messages for Today".

The acknowledgments that appear on page 96 are hereby made a
part of this copyright page.

ISBN 1 84028 027 1

Origination by HBM Print, Singapore
Printed and bound in Italy by L.E.G.O. Spa.

10 9 8 7 6 5 4 3 2 1

The pictures shown on the preliminary pages are:
(page 1) a Catalonian 12th-century painting on wood of Paul;
(page 2) the east portico of the Palaestra in Salamis, Cyprus;
(page 3) a 5th-century ivory diptych carving of Paul; (page 5) Paul
and Barnabas at Lystra, Turkey, in a detail from a 16th-century
stained-glass window from King's College Chapel, England.

CONTENTS

After his conversion, Paul escaped from hostile fellow Jews in Damascus by being lowered in a basket through an opening in a wall, as depicted in this 12th- or 13th-century mosaic from the Monreale Cathedral, Italy.

INTRODUCTION

Inspired man of God, indefatigable missionary, charismatic leader and profound theologian, Paul the Apostle was one of the most influential figures in the history of the early church. He decisively planted the seeds of Christianity in the soil of the Roman Empire and is credited with founding churches in Asia Minor and Europe and with laying out the principles of Christian faith and practice in his letters – the earliest surviving Christian documents.

The account of Paul's life and missionary endeavours is recorded in the New Testament book of Acts, a chronicle believed to have been written by the Gospel writer Luke. Paul himself contributed other important details about his missions in his letters. Born in Tarsus in the Roman province of Cilicia (present-day southeastern Turkey) in about AD 10, Paul was Jewish by birth – a fact he stressed when preaching the Gospel to the Jews – as well as a Roman citizen. In Acts, he is referred to by both his Jewish name, Saul, and its Roman equivalent, Paul.

At an early age, perhaps as a young child, Paul said he was taken to Jerusalem and educated at an academy run by a renowned rabbi named Gamaliel. Later, he became a member of the Pharisees, a Jewish sect known for its strict adherence to the Jewish Law and for its pious living. As he described himself, "I was advancing in Judaism beyond many Jews of my own age and was extremely zealous for the traditions of my fathers [Galatians 1:14]."

✝ Paul discovers Christianity ✝

It is as an enthusiastic Pharisee, hostile to the newly emerged Christian faith, that Paul makes his first appearance in Acts. But during a journey to Damascus in Syria, where he intended to arrest Christians, Paul received a dazzling vision of the living Jesus Christ. As Acts records it, from that time on, Paul dedicated his life to spreading the news of Jesus, crucified and risen.

Paul undertook four journeys: three as a missionary and one as a prisoner. During his three arduous missionary journeys through Asia Minor and Greece – both regions of the Roman Empire – Paul supported himself as a tentmaker. At the time, the empire had almost reached its greatest extent and was divided into provinces governed by

The symbols used at the top of each page represent Paul's journeys: the ship symbolises the first journey; the Corinthian column, the second journey; the Temple of Artemis, the third journey; and the triumphal arch, the final journey.

proconsuls, who were responsible for maintaining a relatively high standard of law and order. Paul and his companions used the network of paved roads that linked the major urban centres and travelled by sea on merchant ships that frequently plied the Mediterranean Sea.

After his third journey, some of Paul's Jewish opponents instigated his arrest by the Romans in Jerusalem. These Jews accused him of undermining the Jewish Law, although Paul consistently presented himself as a faithful Jew, claiming that Christianity was not a threat to Judaism but its fulfilment. As a Roman citizen, Paul had the right to be tried before the emperor at Rome. His "appeal to Caesar" granted, he embarked on his fourth and final journey to present his case in Rome. There, Paul was kept under house arrest for two years while awaiting trial, but he continued to preach the Gospel to his visitors. The book of Acts ends at this point in Paul's history. According to tradition, Paul was executed in Rome during the reign of Emperor Nero (AD 54–68).

† Luke: physician and writer †

Acts, as its preface shows, is a sequel to the third Gospel; both are addressed to Theophilus. The similarity of literary style confirms that the two books are by the same author, and since the second century, church tradition has attributed both books to Paul's "dear friend Luke, the doctor [Colossians 4:14]". Some scholars, however, have questioned the historical accuracy of Acts. They point out discrepancies between Luke's account of Paul's life and character and Paul's own portrait of himself in his letters. For example, Paul's account of what occurred after his conversion and baptism differs from Luke's description in Acts 9:20–26 (pp. 12–13). Also, Luke's suggestion of a degree of harmony between Paul and the Apostle Peter regarding Gentile converts and the Jewish Law (p. 31) seems to conflict with Paul's criticism of Peter on this matter in his letter to the Galatians (2:11–14).

Other scholars emphasise how accurate Luke is regarding the smallest details, such as the titles of Roman officials, and suggest that he was accurate on more important points. Although Luke could not have known directly of some of the events and speeches he reports, he probably drew on reliable sources from the churches of Jerusalem, Caesarea and Antioch. Passages in Acts (16:10–17; 20:6–21:18; and 27:1–28:16) that refer to "we" and "us" instead of "they" and "them" suggest that in these instances Luke was giving a firsthand account of one of Paul's companions, although this may be a literary device. Many scholars believe that this person was Luke himself. In any event, Acts and Paul's letters were written with different aims in mind. Luke wanted to describe how the Gospel spread from Judea to Rome. To do this, he had to select his material carefully, condensing it when necessary. In the manner of ancient historians, Luke may also have constructed speeches to suit his point. Paul, by contrast, wrote to address specific problems of faith and doctrine in the Christian communities.

✝ *The missionary journeys* ✝

This book describes the three missionary journeys of Paul and his final voyage to Rome. Suffering beatings, stonings and imprisonment, he preached to people from all walks of life and on both sides of the Jewish-Gentile divide. He proclaimed, "There can be neither Jew nor Greek…neither slave nor freeman…neither male nor female – for you are all one in Christ Jesus [Galatians 3:28]." His work played a critical role in Christianity's emergence as a major world faith. ■

Paul holds a sword and book, in this 12th-century Catalonian painting. *They represent "the sword of the Spirit…the word of God [Ephesians 6:17]".*

On the ROAD to DAMASCUS

The CONVERSION of SAUL

ACTS 9:1–31

> 66 'Go, for this man is my chosen instrument to bring my name before Gentiles and kings and before the people of Israel.' 99
>
> ACTS 9:15

THE STORY OF how Saul, a devout Jew, became Paul, a Christian evangelist, begins near Damascus. As Saul approached the city, with plans to arrest members of the nascent church, he had a vision that transformed him from a zealous anti-Christian to a passionate preacher of the faith. Luke describes the conversion three times in Acts, and Paul alludes to it in his letters to the churches (Galatians 1; Corinthians).

Saul was one of many Jews who felt that the followers of Jesus posed a threat to the Jewish religion. The tensions at their most extreme are illustrated in the story of Stephen (Acts 6–7). Accused of blasphemy by the Sanhedrin – the supreme council of the Jews – Stephen was stoned to death. As Acts records, Saul "approved of the killing" and himself sent followers of the faith to prison. Later, "breathing threats to slaughter the Lord's disciples", Saul asked the Jewish high priest for permission to arrest "any followers of the faith" in the Syrian city of Damascus, where the Gospel was attracting converts.

Granted permission, Saul left for Damascus. As he approached the city, a "light from heaven" suddenly flashed around him. His travelling companions also saw it and were speechless. Saul sank to his knees and heard a voice say, "Saul, Saul, why are you persecuting me?" When Saul asked who the speaker was, the voice said, "I am Jesus, whom you are persecuting." Jesus instructed Saul to proceed to Damascus. When Saul rose and

opened his eyes, he was blind. For three days, he could not see and did not eat or drink.

In Damascus, a disciple named Ananias had a vision of Jesus telling him to seek out Saul at the "house of Judas", in the street named "Straight". Ananias demurred – Saul was a noted persecutor of the church. Jesus assured Ananias that Saul would spread the faith to the Gentiles and the "people of Israel". Ananias went to Judas's house, explaining that Jesus had sent him so that Saul could regain his sight and be "filled with the Holy Spirit". He laid his hands on Saul, who felt as if "scales" had fallen from his eyes, and he could see again. Saul was then baptised into the church.

Saul began to preach the Gospel in the synagogues of Damascus, inciting some Jews to murderous anger. He was forced to flee the city at night, lowered in a basket outside the city wall, and return to Jerusalem. The disciples there were skeptical of his conversion until Barnabas, a member of the church, convinced them that it was true. Saul continued preaching, and he continued to anger some Jews, this time Greek-speaking Jews, called Hellenists. Again he had to flee, so he went to his hometown of Tarsus in Cilicia.

✝ The vision of Jesus ✝

It is ironic that Saul's sudden conversion to faith in Jesus occurred during his crusade against the faithful in Damascus. Saul intended to arrest Jewish converts to the new faith or possibly to kidnap

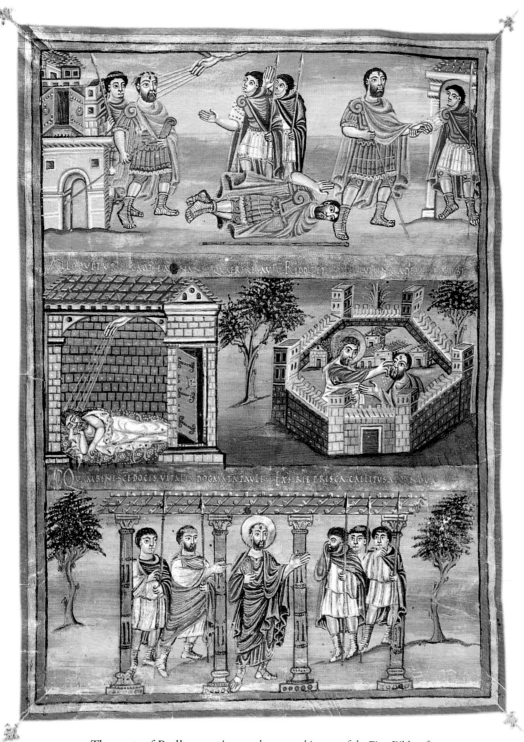

The events of Paul's conversion *are shown on this page of the* First Bible of Charles the Bald *(843–851). It depicts, from the top, Paul's vision, Ananias's vision and his laying hands on Paul, and Paul preaching the Gospel.*

them, since the Sanhedrin did not have legal authority outside Jewish territory. In the late AD 30s, the city itself was either under the jurisdiction of the Roman province of Syria or controlled by Aretas IV, the king of the Nabataean Arabs. It was his governor, or ethnarch, who, Paul claims, tried to prevent him from leaving the city (2 Corinthians 11:32).

In his letter to the Galatians, Paul describes the circumstances of his vision in terms similar to Luke's account. Luke does not say that Saul saw Jesus, only that he was dazzled by the light that "shone all around". He chose a Greek verb that was often used to describe lightning, but it may also suggest that the light was an expression of divine glory. Luke says that Saul saw the light at noon, in clear daylight (Acts 22:6), referred to it as a vision (Acts 26:19), and placed the vision in the same category as Jesus' post-resurrection appearances (1 Corinthians 15:8). Luke also suggests that Saul's vision was not a subjective experience. His companions witnessed the light and dropped to the ground (Acts 22:9 and 26:14).

> ❝ *'I have been sent by the Lord Jesus … so that you may … be filled with the Holy Spirit.'* ❞
>
> ACTS 9:17

After lying stricken for three days in Damascus, Saul was approached by Ananias, who was described by Luke as being "a devout follower of the Law [Acts 22:12]". Despite his original reservations, Ananias greeted Saul as "Brother Saul" and welcomed him into the fellowship, triggering

Cleopatra's gate is an entrance to the city of Tarsus, Paul's birthplace. The gate, which still stands today, is a stone structure built in the period of the Roman Empire.

Basket weaving is still practised in Tarsus today. When Paul fled Damascus, he was lowered through an opening in the city wall in a large basket similar to the almost-complete basket shown here.

the end of Saul's physical and spiritual blindness. With his sight restored, Saul was about to become Paul, "light to the Gentiles [Acts 13:47]".

Luke's account of what happened after Paul's baptism differs in some details from Paul's version in his letters. In Acts, Paul began to preach in Damascus, then, "after some time passed", fled to Jerusalem. In Galatians, however, Paul went to "Arabia", an area east of Palestine, before returning to Damascus. Only after three years did he go to Jerusalem, where he stayed for two weeks. Luke probably condensed some of the events because they were not critical to the point he was making. But Luke and Paul do agree that Paul fled Damascus by means of a basket (2 Corinthians 11:32–33) and later left Jerusalem for Tarsus in Cilicia (Galatians 1:21).

Luke follows Paul's departure to Tarsus with a summary of the church's growth in Judea, Galilee and Samaria, fulfilling the words of Christ that the word of God would be taken across Palestine (Acts 1:8). With Paul's conversion, the stage was set for the spread of the Gospel to the Gentile world. ▪

MESSAGE
— for —
TODAY

"SURPRISED BY JOY" is how the author C. S. Lewis described the sudden experience of Christ's presence in his life. Many Christians, like Paul, have been overwhelmed by the grace of God and have discovered that they could embrace as friends those they had once despised. One Northern Irish Protestant terrorist related how, while in prison for armed robbery, he experienced the love of Christ. Once he accepted God, he was even reconciled with his former enemies, the IRA prisoners.

God's power to change even the most hardened criminal means that no person is beyond repentance and grace, and, therefore, no person should ever be written off as hopeless. It also means that whatever hatred we may harbour in our hearts, we, too, may find our darkness flooded by light and our bitterness changed to compassion.

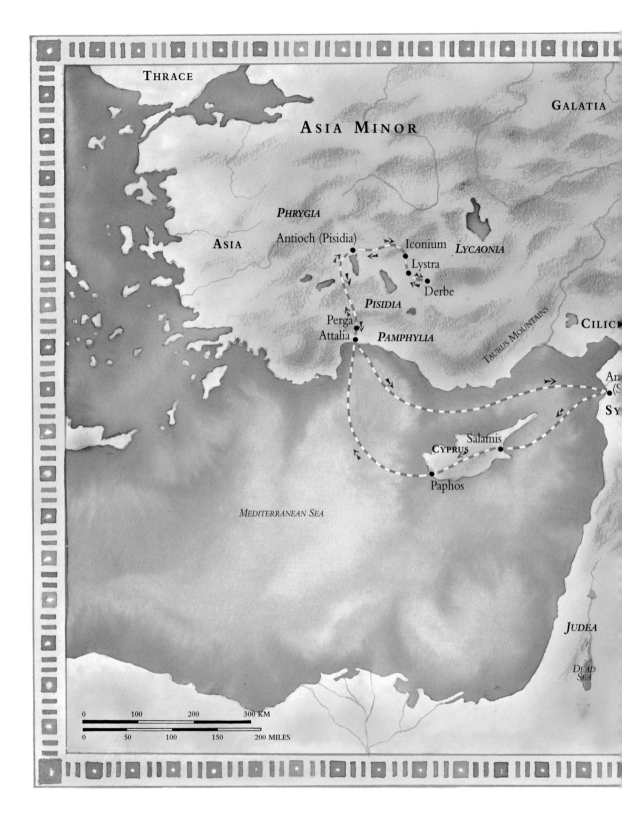

THRACE

ASIA MINOR

GALATIA

PHRYGIA

ASIA

Antioch (Pisidia)

Iconium

LYCAONIA

Lystra

Derbe

PISIDIA

Perga

Attalia

PAMPHYLIA

TAURUS MOUNTAINS

CILIC

An
(S

Sy

Salamis

CYPRUS

Paphos

MEDITERRANEAN SEA

JUDEA

DEAD
SEA

0   100   200   300 KM

0   50   100   150   200 MILES

The first journey began at Antioch in Syria. Paul and his companions travelled from there to Cyprus, Perga and Antioch in Pisidia. They continued to Iconium, Lystra and Derbe, then back to Perga and Antioch in Syria.

THE FIRST MISSIONARY JOURNEY

ACTS 13–14

THE FIRST JOURNEY of Paul and his companion, Barnabas, took them into Asia Minor. As Luke relates in Acts, the young church was at this point established enough to organise a missionary expedition. What makes this first missionary journey particularly significant is that it was the church's first planned venture into Gentile territory. Beforehand, the Gospel had been spread in a haphazard fashion by the efforts of individuals who had escaped from persecution in Jerusalem. With the guidance of the Holy Spirit, the Antioch church in Syria chose Paul and Barnabas as its emissaries and sent them on their way with a formal blessing.

Travelling by land and sea, across rugged and sometimes mountainous country, the two men arrived at remote towns and preached the "word of God" first to the Jewish communities. A Jew himself, Paul believed Jesus was the long-awaited Jewish Messiah. But he often encountered hostility from the Jews, perhaps because they felt that he was undermining their own religion. Only when rejected by the Jews did Paul turn to the Gentiles, among whom he and Barnabas found many new followers for the faith.

Paul's radical message of salvation through Jesus Christ, however, could provoke and antagonise Gentiles as well as Jews. In the town of Iconium, for example, Paul and Barnabas escaped a stoning. In Lystra, Paul was not as fortunate – he was stoned unconscious. Nevertheless, the two men continued braving danger and overcoming hardships to establish new churches throughout Asia Minor. ■

The FALSE PROPHET

The MISSIONARIES DEPART for CYPRUS

ACTS 13:1–12

" So it was that after fasting and prayer they laid
their hands on them and sent them off. "

ACTS 13:3

A FTER PAUL'S DRAMATIC conversion and his first episodes of preaching the Gospel, Luke records that the Jewish Christians of Jerusalem sent Paul home to Tarsus. It was Barnabas, the disciple responsible for convincing his fellow followers of the faith that Paul had genuinely converted (Acts 9:27), who found Paul in Tarsus and brought him to Antioch in Syria (p. 90). Together, Paul and Barnabas remained in Antioch for a year, teaching and strengthening the church. In this city, Luke says, Jesus' followers were first called Christians.

According to Acts, Paul and Barnabas left Antioch on at least one occasion to deliver a relief fund to Jerusalem in anticipation of an imminent famine – an event that was predicted by a Christian prophet, or preacher, named Agabus (Acts 11:27–30). When they returned to Antioch, the two disciples brought with them John Mark, the traditional author of one of the four Gospels, whom they would take as their "assistant" on their forthcoming journey.

† Paul and Barnabas are sent off †

With the church firmly established in Antioch in Syria – Luke is able to name its prominent leaders as Barnabas, Simeon "called Niger", Lucius of Cyrene, Manaen and Paul – the time was evidently ripe for the message of the Gospel to be taken farther afield. Luke records that one day while members of the church were worshipping and fasting, the Holy Spirit spoke to them. Presumably using one of the faithful as a mouthpiece, the Holy Spirit said, "I want Barnabas and Saul set apart for the work to which I have called them [Acts 13:2]."

After they had finished their prayers and fasting, the Antioch disciples formally blessed Paul and Barnabas by the laying on of hands and sent them on their first missionary journey. It began with a voyage to the island of Cyprus, lying some 210 km (130 miles) away from Seleucia, the port of Antioch in Syria where they were based. The port of Salamis on Cyprus was their first stop. There, they taught "the word of God" in the synagogues of the Jewish community. Next, they travelled to the city of Paphos, 150 km (90 miles) to the southwest. In this city, they encountered Bar-Jesus, also called Elymas. This Jewish "magician and false prophet" had attached himself to the entourage of the island's Roman governor, Sergius Paulus.

Intrigued by the arrival of the two itinerant preachers, Sergius asked Paul and Barnabas to speak to him about the word of God. Bar-Jesus, however, feared that he would lose his influence if his employer was converted to the Christian faith and tried to stop them. Inspired by the Holy Spirit, Paul – only at this point in Acts does Luke use this name instead of Saul – looked Bar-Jesus in the face and denounced him as a fraud, a son of the devil, and one who twisted the "straightforward ways of the Lord". He told him that the

Within the tapestry image:

L·SERGIVS PAVLLVS
ASIAE PROCOS:
CHRISTIANAM FIDEM
AMPLECTITVR
SAVLI PREDICATIONE

"hand of the Lord" would strike him and that he would be blinded for a period of time. Right after the utterance of these words, Bar-Jesus's vision went "misty and dark", and he was forced to beg for someone to lead him by the hand. Profoundly impressed by what he had just witnessed, Sergius immediately became a believer.

Bar-Jesus the false prophet is shown being struck blind by the red-robed Paul, in this detail from the Brussels Tapestries. The Roman governor Sergius Paulus, seated, witnesses the event.

✝ Compelling evidence ✝

Cyprus, an island about 225 km (140 miles) long and 100 km (60 miles) wide, had been made a Roman province under the jurisdiction of the Roman senate in 22 BC. Renowned for its ship-building and copper mining, it would certainly have supported a large community. The size of this community, along with the fact that Barnabas came from Cyprus (Acts 4:36), may explain, in part, why it was the first stop for the disciples on their mission.

At the port of Salamis, Paul and Barnabas, accompanied by John Mark, established the pattern for later missions by going first to the Jewish

At Paphos, Cyprus, where Paul encountered Bar-Jesus, stands the Church of the Blessed Virgin Mary of the Golden City. According to local tradition, Paul was tied to one of the pillars in front of the church and flogged.

community and preaching to them, then addressing the Gentiles. At Paphos, the capital of the island, the two men may have preached for some time before being summoned by Sergius Paulus, whom Luke describes as "extremely intelligent".

Bar-Jesus was most likely either an astrologer or a fortune-teller employed by Sergius. The other name given to him, Elymas – which is Greek for "magician" – may stem from an Arabic word that means "wise" or "skilful". In any case, Bar-Jesus realised that his livelihood might be jeopardised, so he tried to prevent Paul and

Barnabas from converting Sergius (Luke does not state how). Paul was "filled with the Holy Spirit" and responded with inspired anger, subsequently cursing Bar-Jesus for his attempt to pervert the course of God's word. Bar-Jesus's resulting blindness was not, Luke suggests, a permanent condition, and Luke may have intended his readers to associate it with Paul's own temporary blindness after his conversion (pp. 10–13).

Sergius witnessed these events with amazement and became a believer. Ironically, in his attempt to prevent such an outcome, Bar-Jesus incited Paul's wrath, which may have instigated the most compelling evidence. Some scholars have pointed out that Luke does not say that Sergius was baptised, perhaps suggesting that the Roman was not willing to commit himself totally to the church. Nevertheless, Luke illustrates that high-standing Roman officials were among those who received the Gospel message with interest and conversion. Meanwhile, Paul and Barnabas made preparations to cross to the mainland of Asia Minor to continue their work.

> ❝ *'Now watch how the hand of the Lord will strike you: you will be blind, and for a time you will not see the sun.'* ❞
>
> ACTS 13:11

From this time on, Luke refers to Paul solely by his Roman name, perhaps because it was more in keeping with Paul's presence in the wider Gentile world. While previously Luke had usually named Barnabas before Paul when describing their actions, at this point he reverses the order, suggesting that Paul was becoming the dominant member of the partnership. ∎

This harbour wall at Seleucia – the port of Antioch in Syria – is where Paul and Barnabas purportedly set sail to the first destination of their mission, Cyprus.

MESSAGE — *for* — TODAY

IN A WORLD FULL OF competing modern gurus, many people find it difficult to know where to turn for spiritual guidance. The problem of "false prophets" is at least as old as the history recorded in the Bible. Paul's condemnation of Bar-Jesus may appear intolerant of the beliefs and practices of others. Yet a false teacher can lead innocent seekers into a destructive misty darkness.

Jesus said that we can recognise true and false prophets by their fruits – the motivation and results of their work (Matthew 7:16). False teachers seek fame, money and power; but true teachers, as Paul wrote in his letter to the Corinthians, use their gifts "for the general good". False teachers create confusion, despair and self-centredness; genuine teachers lead people to "faith, hope, and love…and the greatest of them is love [1 Corinthians 13:13]".

PREACHING to JEWS and GOD-FEARERS

PAUL and BARNABAS at ANTIOCH in PISIDIA
ACTS 13:13–52

> " *'My brothers, sons of Abraham's race, and all you God-fearers,*
> *this message of salvation is meant for you.'* "
> ### ACTS 13:26

AFTER THEIR STAY on Cyprus, Paul, Barnabas and John Mark headed for Asia Minor, entering the next stage of their journey. From the city of Paphos they sailed 240 km (150 miles) across the Mediterranean Sea to the Bay of Attalia, and from there they made their way to Perga, in the low-lying, marshy region of Pamphylia.

Luke says that at this point in the journey, John Mark left the missionaries to go back to Jerusalem. Luke gives no reason, but some commentators suggest that John Mark may have been reluctant to take the Gospel to Gentiles. The fact that Paul would later hold the action against the young man indicates that John Mark's decision was not well received (Acts 15:37–39). Without stopping to preach the word of God in Perga, the disciples embarked on a 130-km (80-mile) trek through rugged, bandit-infested territory to Antioch in Pisidia (p. 90).

As he had done on Cyprus, Paul first established contact with the Jewish community. One Sabbath, at a synagogue service, he accepted an invitation to speak to the congregation, a group that included both Jews and God-fearers – that is, Gentiles who respected the Jewish religion but who had not converted to it. Rising to his feet and motioning for silence with his hand, Paul addressed his audience.

He began by rehearsing with the crowd the early history of Israel. He spoke of how God led the Israelites out of Egypt and brought them through the desert to the Promised Land of Canaan; how God gave his people a succession of leaders known as "judges"; and how, after this period, the people demanded a king. God responded by giving them first Saul and then David, from whose line God promised to send a Messiah, the one who would bring salvation to the world. Paul then announced that God had fulfilled this promise of a Messiah in Jesus, whose coming was foretold by the preachings of John the Baptist.

✝ Proclaiming the "good news" ✝

In the second half of his sermon, Paul assured his listeners that the salvation brought by Jesus was meant for each of them. He described how the people of Jerusalem had not recognised the spiritual status of Jesus and had executed him. They had not realised, Paul explained, that by taking these actions, they were fulfilling the scriptures (Psalm 118:22 and Isaiah 53). God raised Jesus from the dead, and "for many days" He appeared to his closest followers.

Paul went on to say that he and Barnabas had come to Antioch precisely to proclaim this "good news" – that God had fulfilled his promise to the

Jews in the person of Jesus. To back up this claim, Paul quoted from several sections of the scriptures (Psalms 2:7 and 16:10; Isaiah 55:3). He also stressed that Jesus, "whom God had raised up", had not suffered any "corruption", or decay, after his death. Paul continued his sermon by stating that only through Jesus could peoples' sins be forgiven. "Every believer" could be "justified", or acquitted of their sins in a way that was not possible through the Law of Moses, the Jewish Law. Finally, he warned his audience about the perils of ignoring his words, and he cited the words of the prophet Habakkuk, "I am doing something in your own days which you will not believe if you are told of it [Habakkuk 1:5]."

Paul's sermon must have caused great interest. The people invited him to preach the following Sabbath, and when the time came, the synagogue

Paul arguing with the Jews is depicted on this enamel tablet, part of an English retable (a raised shelf that is positioned over an altar), dating from c.1180.

was packed. However, a number of the Jews present "were filled with jealousy" and contradicted what Paul said with "blasphemies". In response, Paul and Barnabas said that they had been determined to proclaim God's word to them, the Jews, first; now they would turn to the Gentiles. Luke records that when the Gentiles heard them, they were delighted and gave thanks to God. In this way, Luke says, the Gospel "spread through the whole countryside".

The Jews, however, retaliated. They persuaded some of Antioch's influential people, among them, probably, "leading men" and the wives of the city's magistrates, that Paul and Barnabas were making trouble. The strategy worked, and the two men were expelled from the town. Shaking the dust off their feet – a gesture that showed dismissal – Paul and Barnabas departed for Iconium.

✝ Turning to the Gentiles ✝

Paul's address to the people of Antioch is the only one of his sermons addressed to a Jewish audience that is recorded in detail in Acts. In this way, Luke established what Paul would typically have said on such an occasion. When he mentions Paul preaching a sermon to the Jews elsewhere, his readers can thus surmise its content.

Some scholars have pointed out that in structure and material, Paul's speech resembles those given by the disciples Peter and Stephen earlier on in Acts (2:14–36 and 7:1–53, respectively). As a result, some have questioned the extent to which these speeches are historical and how much they owe to Luke's literary skills. Conversely, many scholars now think that early Christian preachers modelled their speeches to some extent on those given by contemporary Jewish rabbis. This may explain why they display a common structure.

This Hellenistic city wall and tower would have greeted Paul and Barnabas at Perga, the city from which John Mark left the missionaries to return to Jersualem.

In modern-day Pisidia, Turkey, nomad women can be found milking sheep. This herd grazes above Lake Egridir, near Antioch. Paul probably crossed the Karakus Mountains, in the background, on his later journeys.

Paul's sermon seems to complement the speech given by Stephen, who, when addressing the Sanhedrin shortly before his martyrdom, also rehearsed the early history of Israel. While Stephen concentrated on Abraham, the Patriarchs, and Moses, however, Paul focused on the period of David and the monarchy. Luke may have deliberately chosen to emphasise different parts of the two speeches to avoid repetition. In addition, Stephen and Paul had pursued different aims: Stephen warned his listeners, "You stubborn people… You are always resisting the Holy Spirit [Acts 7:51]"; Paul, by linking Jesus with David, conveyed the idea that God's promise of sending a Messiah had been fulfilled.

> **The next Sabbath almost the whole town assembled to hear the word of God.**
> ACTS 13:44

Like Stephen's speech, Paul's sermon had a powerful effect on those who heard it. It also aroused hostility and jealousy among a number of Jews, although Luke does not say why. Perhaps it was because they disliked the Gentiles' being welcomed into the church with the same enthusiasm as themselves, "God's chosen people". Or perhaps they feared that Paul's success in attracting Gentile God-fearers would break down the distinction between Jews and Gentiles.

In any case, the Jews' opposition strengthened Paul and Barnabas in their conviction that they must turn their efforts to the Gentiles. To this effect, the two men "spoke out fearlessly", quoting from the prophet Isaiah to support their message. "I shall make you a light to the nations so that my salvation may reach the remotest parts of Earth [Isaiah 49:6]." Paul and Barnabas set out for their next destination, leaving behind both numerous Jews who were incensed by their words and new converts – presumably, mostly Gentiles – who were "filled with joy and the Holy Spirit".

MESSAGE
—for—
TODAY

GOD'S MERCY TO US should not be regarded as a private blessing but rather as a call to serve others. In Paul's case, his conversion also marked a commitment to preach to the Gentiles. Many Jews believed that Israel, by its faithfulness to God's Law, was intended to be a "light to the nations [Isaiah 49:6]". But to some Jews, who had been raised on the notion that "the chosen people" were called to be separate, Paul's proclamation of God's gift of eternal life to the Gentiles sounded like blasphemy.

Throughout history, people have discriminated against those of other religions, races, classes or gender. Paul's message that in Christ "there can be neither Jew nor Greek…slave nor freemam…male nor female [Galatians 3:28]" is as relevant today as it was in Antioch in Pisidia nearly 2,000 years ago.

An ESCAPE from STONING

The GOSPEL REACHES ICONIUM
ACTS 14:1–7

> " *…they went to the Jewish synagogue…and they spoke so effectively that a great many Jews and Greeks became believers.* "
> ACTS 14:1

H OUNDED FROM Antioch in Pisidia, Paul and Barnabas left for the city of Iconium (p. 90). When they arrived, the two made themselves known to the Jewish community and were invited to speak in the synagogue. According to Luke, many of the congregation converted to the Gospel. But a core group of Jews who were unimpressed by the missionaries' message "stirred up the Gentiles against the brothers and set them in opposition [Acts 14:2]".

At first, the "opposition" apparently consisted of verbal abuse, such as jeers and shouting, when Paul and Barnabas were preaching. But the two men stayed "for some time", continuing to preach fearlessly. They also performed "signs and wonders", probably acts of healing and exorcisms, through God's power.

Luke says that the people were polarised by the conflict between Paul and Barnabas and their Jewish opponents. The anti-Christian party prevailed. With the permission of the "authorities",

The city of Iconium, illustrated in this 1840 engraving by W. M. Bartlett, stood on a plateau above a fertile plain with meandering mountain streams.

a number of Jews and Gentiles plotted to attack and stone the two men. Informed of the threat to their safety, the disciples decided that it was time to continue their journey.

† The synagogue congregation †

The events at Iconium mirror what happened at Antioch in Pisidia – preliminary success followed by hostility from the Jews. On their arrival in the town, Paul and Barnabas first visited the Jewish community and their synagogue. For the Jews of the Diaspora – those who were "dispersed" from their homeland – the synagogue was the centre of their lives, serving as a place of worship, a courthouse, a schoolhouse and a meeting place. At the Sabbath service in the synagogue, Paul's audience would at least respond to someone with a shared religious background. Retelling Jewish history and citing the scriptures, as he did at Antioch in Pisidia (pp. 20–23), Paul emphasised this common ground.

Apart from the Jews, members of the congregation included proselytes, or Gentiles who embraced the Jewish religion – including the rites of circumcision and sacrifice – and God-fearers, who admired the monotheism and ethical teachings of Judaism. From these two groups came most of Paul's converts. Although they had studied the Jewish Law and scriptures and knew of the Jews' hopes for a Messiah, they were regarded by the Jews as "second-class citizens".

It is not surprising that the God-fearers were attracted to Paul's message, which proclaimed that through Jesus the distinction between Jew and Gentile was abolished. This may have been the issue that enraged some of the Jews. A number of them incited Gentiles and other Jews against Paul and Barnabas. At first, the two men stayed to carry on their work. But eventually, they realised that the authorities – the Jewish leaders, town magistrates, or both – were ready to turn a blind eye to what would have amounted to a stoning. So they left to take their message elsewhere. ▪

MESSAGE
—for—
TODAY

PAUL WAS NO COWARD. He spoke boldly in the name of Jesus and, as a result, suffered much persecution. He did not, however, seek martyrdom. Whenever opponents put his life in danger, Paul moved on to another city. Like the Dalai Lama, who fled from Tibet in 1959 to escape from the repressive Chinese authorities, Paul believed that he would be of more use proclaiming his message throughout the world than being stoned to death.

Although we should never betray our convictions, sometimes discretion is the better part of valour. Taking a stand based on a deeply held belief is almost certain to stir up some hostility in others who may have different opinions. Knowing when to make a judicious retreat may allow us – like Paul – to be more effective in the long run.

MISTAKEN for GODS

The DISCIPLES at LYSTRA

ACTS 14:8–20

*" Paul looked at him intently and saw that
he had the faith to be cured. "*

ACTS 14:9

LYSTRA WAS A remote outpost of the Roman Empire (p. 90). Paul and Barnabas sought refuge there after the mounting threat to their lives had driven them from Iconium, approximately 30 km (20 miles) to the northeast.

On one occasion, as Paul preached to the Lystrans, probably in the marketplace, a man who had been unable to walk from birth caught Paul's attention. Paul could see that the man had the requisite faith to be healed, so he shouted to him to stand up. Immediately, the man "jumped up" and started to walk around.

The effect of Paul's miracle on the onlookers was dramatic. Shouting excitedly in their local Lycaonian dialect, they declared that Paul and Barnabas must be gods. They identified Barnabas with Zeus, the king of the Greek pantheon, and Paul with Hermes, the messenger god (because "Paul was the principal speaker"). The local pagan priests then proposed making a ritual sacrifice to Paul and Barnabas, and led out oxen adorned with ceremonial garlands for the offering.

Paul and Barnabas were shocked at this unexpected development. To express their revulsion, they tore their clothes in symbolic disgust and rushed into the crowd of their would-be worshippers. One of them – most likely Paul – then addressed the throng, insisting that they were not gods but mortals. In fact, their express purpose in coming to Lystra, he said, was to proclaim the good news about Jesus Christ, to turn the people

from their pagan deities and "empty idols" to the "living God who made sky and Earth and the sea and all that these hold [Acts 14:15]".

Paul explained that in the past God excused the Gentiles' ignorance of God's laws. But he also said that there was enough evidence in the natural world for people to infer God's existence. It was God who sent the rain, made the crops grow, and provided food. But even with this impassioned speech, Paul barely managed to stop the sacrifice.

At some point, hostile Jews from Antioch in Pisidia and Iconium arrived in town and began to poison the minds of the Lystrans against the two men. Once again, their tactics worked; the people stoned Paul and, believing he was dead, dumped his body beyond the town walls. As "the disciples", probably Lystran converts, crowded around his body, Paul came to his senses, stood up and walked back into town. Seeing the man whom they believed to be dead walking toward them, the mob must have wondered if he really was a god. The next day, Paul and Barnabas left for Derbe, 130 km (80 miles) to the east.

✝ Persuading the pagans ✝

In the history of Paul's missionary work, Lystra stands out as the first town he visited with no established Jewish community or synagogue. Paul and Barnabas began immediately to preach to the pagan townsfolk, understanding that these individuals were ignorant of the Jewish scriptures and

Paul curing a cripple *is shown in this stained-glass window from a church in Norwich, Norfolk. Barnabas stands beside him.*

unsympathetic to the idea of worshipping one God. To the missionaries' amazement, they discovered that they themselves were being hailed as Greek pagan gods.

> ❝ *We have come with good news to make you turn from these empty idols to the living God.* ❞
>
> ACTS 14:15

Some modern scholars doubt that the Lystrans were really naive enough to mistake the missionaries for Greek immortals. The Roman poet Ovid, however, recorded a legend that Zeus and Hermes – he used their Latin names Jupiter and Mercury – did once visit the locality of Lystra. These two deities visited an old couple called Philemon and Baucis, who were the only people in the area to offer them hospitality. Consequently, the gods slaughtered the entire population of the region except for Philemon and Baucis, whom they made guardians of their temple.

Modern archaeological evidence has shown that a cult of these two gods did exist near Lystra into the AD third century. Perhaps the Lystrans, steeped in their local legends, wanted to avoid the possibility of

Zeus, the chief deity in the Greek pantheon, is portrayed in this Hellenistic statue. He is often depicted as a sky god with a thunderbolt.

divine retribution from failing to recognise and honour Paul and Barnabas as gods – after all, they were capable of performing miracles, like the gods of the Lystran legend.

Faced with this superstitious, volatile and uneducated audience, Paul had to tailor his message accordingly. There was no point, for example, in mentioning Abraham, Moses or David, since these people did not know the Jewish religion. First, he had to establish that there was only one "living God", who had overlooked the Gentiles' ignorance of Him in the past. Paul implied, however, that with the arrival of the Gospel, the people were without an excuse for their lack of knowledge. He later stated this theme in his letter to the Romans (1:18–23). Paul then argued that the existence of the one God could be found in the evidence around them. He spoke to the Lystrans of the natural cycle of nature, the beneficence of rain and the productivity of the land. Only a "living God", and not their "empty idols", he proclaimed, could create such "good things".

Before the Lystrans could assimilate the implications of Paul's words, a group of Jews hostile to the missionaries succeeded in stirring up the people against both Paul and Barnabas. Paul was evidently lucky to survive the violent stoning, almost certainly the incident that he referred to in 2 Corinthians (11:25). Luke says further that the "disciples came crowding around him", showing that Paul's missionary efforts had not been completely in vain.

Two oxen are harnessed to a plough typical of the Aegean region. In Paul's day, oxen were valued as work animals and represented wealth. They would be slaughtered only on special occasions, such as a pagan sacrifice.

The next day, Paul and Barnabas left for Derbe, where they preached without opposition. At this point they must have decided that they had come to the end of the road on this mission and decided to return home. They retraced their steps through the towns they had visited, where they gave new heart to the recently converted disciples and appointed elders, or leaders, to head the communities. Back in Perga in Pamphylia, the two men proclaimed the Gospel before making their way to the port of Attalia, from which they set sail for Antioch in Syria. At home, they met with their fellow worshippers and told them about their journey – the miracles, the escapes and how God had "opened the door of faith to the Gentiles". ▪

MESSAGE
—for—
TODAY

WE MAY NOT TREAT people as gods in the modern world, but the media are quick to idolise successful athletes, social celebrities and film stars. Like the fickle crowd at Lystra, which one day treated Paul and Barnabas as gods and the next day stoned them, the media can just as quickly turn against yesterday's idols.

Conversely, people at the peak of their fame and success may find it difficult to remember that they are only human beings. For Christians, positions of authority and the attention of the media are lent by God to serve godly purposes, not to glorify the self.

Leading God-centred lives should guide us to be more aware of our own human limitations. In proper humility, we can avoid inappropriately glorifying our heroes and leaders and turn, instead, to faithful, responsible service.

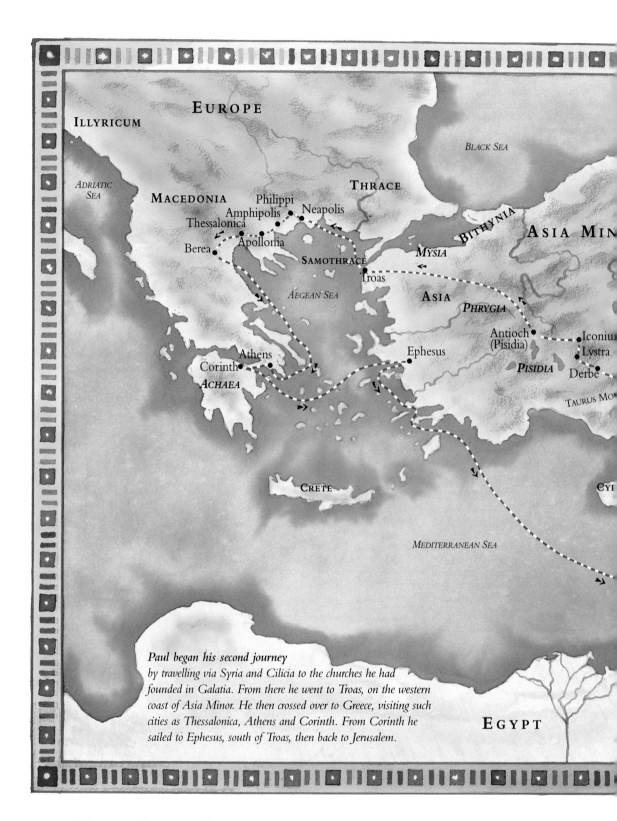

EUROPE

ILLYRICUM

ADRIATIC
SEA

MACEDONIA

Thessalonica

Berea

Apollonia

Amphipolis

Philippi

Neapolis

THRACE

BLACK SEA

BITHYNIA

ASIA MIN

MYSIA

SAMOTHRACE

Troas

AEGEAN SEA

ASIA

PHRYGIA

Antioch
(Pisidia)

Iconiu

Lystra

Athens

Corinth

ACHAEA

Ephesus

PISIDIA

Derbe

TAURUS MO

CRETE

MEDITERRANEAN SEA

CY

Paul began his second journey
by travelling via Syria and Cilicia to the churches he had
founded in Galatia. From there he went to Troas, on the western
coast of Asia Minor. He then crossed over to Greece, visiting such
cities as Thessalonica, Athens and Corinth. From Corinth he
sailed to Ephesus, south of Troas, then back to Jerusalem.

EGYPT

GALATIA

CILICIA

Tarsus

SYRIA

Antioch
(Syria)

PHOENICIA

Sidon

Tyre

Ptolemais

Caesarea

JUDEA

Jerusalem

DEAD
SEA

0   100   200   300 KM

0   50   100   150   200 MILES

THE SECOND MISSIONARY JOURNEY

ACTS 15:36–18:23

WHEN PAUL AND BARNABAS returned to Antioch in Syria, they reported on how God was accepted by the Gentiles. Meanwhile, some Jewish Christians began to teach that Gentile believers must be circumcised – in accordance with Jewish Law – to join the community of believers. This began a controversy that appears to have been settled by a church council in Jerusalem (Acts 15). Luke gives more importance to this council than Paul himself does in his letter (Galatians 2).

The disciple Peter argued against circumcision, saying that God welcomed the Gentiles and gave them the Holy Spirit. Paul and Barnabas backed Peter with news of their successful mission to the Gentiles. James, Jesus' brother, proposed excusing the Gentiles from circumcision but suggested that they comply with parts of the Law to allow fellowship between Jewish and Gentile believers. They should abstain from "illicit marriages", the meat of animals killed in pagan sacrifice, and the meat and blood of strangled animals. The council ratified the proposal in a letter sent to Antioch with Paul, Barnabas and two Christians from Jerusalem, Judas Barsabbas and Silas. They gave it to the faithful, who "were delighted with the encouragement it gave them [Acts 15:31]".

In Antioch, bolstered by the council's decision, Paul suggested a second missionary journey to Barnabas. But an argument between them ended with each man going his separate way. Paul set off on a three-year mission, his second journey, to spread the Gospel in Europe. ∎

The CALLING of TIMOTHY

PAUL, SILAS and TIMOTHY ENTER MACEDONIA

ACTS 15:36–16:10

" 'Let us go back and visit the brothers in all the towns where we preached the word of the Lord…' "

ACTS 15:36

FTER THE COUNCIL of Jerusalem made the landmark decision to allow Gentiles to join the ranks of the faithful without being circumcised (p. 31), Paul and Barnabas continued to preach the Gospel in Antioch in Syria. At some point, Paul suggested to Barnabas that they return to the towns of Galatia to see how the newly founded churches were faring. Barnabas agreed and proposed taking John Mark along as their companion. But Paul balked at this idea; the memory of Mark's desertion in Perga (p. 20) clearly still upset him. The two men had a "sharp disagreement" and could not be reconciled on the matter, so they "parted company". Barnabas sailed to Cyprus, taking Mark with him, while Paul set off with Silas, a disciple who had travelled from Jerusalem to Antioch after the council.

Paul made his way through Syria and Cilicia, his home province, "consolidating the churches". He then travelled westward through the mountainous pass known as the Cilician Gates to Derbe, and then to Lystra, where he and Barnabas had been mistaken for gods (pp. 26–29). There, he met a Christian named Timothy, a young man born of a Jewish mother and a Greek father, who was well regarded by the local church. Paul, too, was impressed by the youth and recruited him as a travelling companion. First, however, he thought it best that Timothy should be circumcised "on account of the Jews in the locality where everyone knew his father was a Greek".

After leaving Lystra, the missionary group made its way through a number of towns, telling the local Christians of the decisions made at the Jerusalem council. They eventually ventured into "Phrygia and the Galatian country" because the Holy Spirit had made clear to them "not to preach the word in Asia", the Roman province that lay to the west of Galatia. Instead, they headed north toward the province of Bithynia, which bordered the southern shore of the Black Sea. Again, they were discouraged from pursuing their intended course, this time by the "Spirit of Jesus". So the missionaries went through the region of Mysia to the west, arriving at the town of Troas on the Aegean coast of Asia Minor.

One night, while they were staying in Troas, Paul had a vision in which a man from Macedonia, an area of northern Greece, urged him to, "Come across to Macedonia and help us." The vision was decisive. In Luke's accounts, he recorded that Paul and his companions made immediate arrangements to travel to Macedonia, believing that God had called them there to spread the Gospel.

✝ The split with Barnabas ✝

Paul's second missionary journey began with his disagreement with Barnabas over John Mark, who was a relation of Barnabas's. Paul was unwilling to risk another defection by Mark and would not shift from his position. The split

between the two men led to two missions, with Barnabas and Mark going to Cyprus. This is the last mention of them in Acts, but Paul later commended John Mark, calling him a "useful helper in my work [2 Timothy 4:11]". Paul now becomes the principal actor in Acts.

With the blessing of the Antioch Christians, Paul left with Silas – who was a prominent disciple and probably a Roman citizen – on his own

Timothy (right), Paul's new travelling companion, is shown conversing with Paul in this 14th-century rendering from Guiart Desmulins's Bible Historiale.

mission and eventually arrived in Lystra. There, the two men enlisted the services of Timothy, whose mother was a convert from Paul's previous journey. But before they set out again, Paul decided that Timothy should be circumcised. By

Jewish law (Ezra 10:2), marriage between the Jews and the Gentiles was forbidden. However, if a mixed marriage did take place, the offspring were considered to be Jews and the sons were circumcised. (It is not clear whether the mother had to be Jewish in Paul's time, which is the rule today.) For some reason, however, Timothy had not been circumcised. So Paul decided that it would be prudent for Timothy to undergo the ritual to preempt any objections that might arise from the local Jews.

To many scholars, Paul's action is inconsistent with his view that Gentile converts did not have to be circumcised, which he expressed in his letters (for example, Galatians 5:3). Others argue that the difference in Timothy's case was that he was legally a Jew, not a Gentile. For Paul, the ritual was really a matter of expediency, not principle. Timothy's reputation for piety could be compromised among the Jews whom they would encounter in the area. This, in turn, could distract Jewish listeners from the central purpose of the missionaries' work – spreading the Gospel.

The Taurus Mountains would have to be crossed before Paul could reach Derbe from Tarsus. Trekking over its rugged terrain was just one of many physical challenges that Paul endured during his missions.

Galatia and Bithynia, among others. Within these provinces were old ethnic regions, such as Phrygia, Mysia and Galatia (the last a region in the province of the same name, where the Celtic Galatian people originally settled).

Paul planned to enter the province of Asia, which extended along the coast of Asia Minor. But Luke states that the Holy Spirit told Paul not to go, perhaps with a vision or a prophetic utterance. Again, at the frontier of the region of Mysia, northwest of Asia, Paul was warned not to continue toward Bithynia. Luke makes clear in his account that Paul's mission was directed by God.

Finally, at Troas, Paul received in a vision instructions for the next part of his missionary journey. Some scholars have speculated that the man who beckoned Paul to Macedonia may have been Luke, who possibly came from Macedonia (although the man may have been the Macedonian king and general Alexander the Great). One reason given is that in this section of Acts, Luke for the first time suddenly switches from using the pronouns *he* and *they* to *we*.

Scholars have called Acts 16:10–17 and some of the later verses the "we passages" of Acts, and they continue to debate the significance of these

† The call to Macedonia †

With Timothy now in tow, Paul and Silas struck out westward from Lystra and neighbouring Iconium. Luke is vague about their route to Troas. Asia Minor (now Turkey) was divided into various Roman provinces – Asia, passages. Some have proposed that the use of "we" is simply a literary device to make the story more immediate. Other scholars believe that Luke was drawing on a firsthand account of one of Paul's companions but failed to alter the construction from the first to the third person.

> " *We lost no time in arranging a passage to Macedonia, convinced that God had called us to bring them the good news.* "
>
> ACTS 16:10

Many commentators, however, believe that the "we" is Luke's clue to his readers that he was involved in the events described. The change of pronoun would then indicate that Luke, unlike Timothy and Silas, was not a constant companion of Paul's, but joined him for part of the journey. In any event, Paul stood at the threshold of Europe, ready to bring the Gospel into the heartland of ancient Greece. ∎

St. Peter's Church, attached to a cave in Mount Silpius, Antioch, Syria, is purported to be the first established Christian church. Paul may have stopped here on his second journey. The altar shown below is in the cave.

MESSAGE — *for* — TODAY

WHEN OUR PLANS are thwarted, we often grumble or feel discouraged. We seldom consider that God's spirit may be preventing us from going down a blind alley or even directing us to a new approach. For Paul, frustrated plans bespoke the Holy Spirit's guidance and led to a new vision of what he should do. Paul understood that the man's beckoning him to Macedonia was God's way of telling him to take the Gospel to Europe.

It is good to make plans, but it is equally important to be open to new opportunities when plans fall through. A loving God can use bad weather, the loss of a job, conflicts with others, even the death of a loved one, to move us forward on our spiritual journey. When we respond in faith, we can discover the opportunities and deeper meaning God has for us.

DELIVERANCE from PRISON

The MISSIONARIES in PHILIPPI
ACTS 16:11–40

❝ *Suddenly there was an earthquake that shook the prison to its foundations.* **❞**
ACTS 16:26

FROM TROAS, PAUL and his companions set sail northwestward, obeying Paul's vision that God's word should be delivered by them to Macedonia, in northern Greece. They reached the port of Neapolis via the island of Samothrace, then travelled 15 km (10 miles) inland and reached their first destination – Philippi.

Luke implies that no synagogue existed in town where the missionaries could contact the local Jews. So, after a few days, Paul and his group decided to visit a riverside spot outside the city, where they had seen women go to pray. When they arrived, one of the women, a purple-dye trader named Lydia, showed interest in their message of salvation. Then and there, "the Lord opened her heart to accept what Paul was saying". She and her household were baptised into the faith, and she insisted that the Christians use her house during their stay.

Some time after Lydia's conversion, a slave girl began to follow Paul around. Possessed by a spirit that enabled her to predict the future, she earned a great deal of money for her owners as a fortune-teller. Just as the possessed people that Jesus encountered had shouted (Matthew 8:29), the girl continually shouted out that the missionaries were "servants of the Most High God" and had come to tell people how they could be saved. In the end, Paul was so exasperated by her relentless shouting that he ordered the spirit to come out of her in the name of Jesus Christ.

✝ Imprisonment ✝

The slave girl's masters, furious at their financial loss (she could not predict the future without the spirit) dragged Paul and Silas into the marketplace and accused them before the magistrates of creating a disturbance. Appealing to anti-Jewish prejudice, they complained that the two "Jews" were advocating practices that were unlawful for "Romans to accept"; under Roman law, it was illegal for Jews to proselytise. Faced with a hostile mob, the magistrates ordered Paul and Silas to be stripped and flogged. Paul records this "rough treatment and insults" in 1 Thessalonians (2:2). They were thrown into the town's "inner prison", where a jailer chained the two men to the wall and put their feet in stocks.

That night, however, while Paul and Silas were "praying and singing God's praises", the town was struck by an earthquake. The prison shook, its doors flew open, and the prisoners' chains fell from the walls. Seeing the open doors, the jailer panicked and prepared to kill himself because he knew that, by law, he would have to bear the punishment if any prisoner escaped. However,

Paul shouted to him that no one had left. Apparently, so great was the jailer's relief that he threw himself at the feet of Paul and Silas.

The jailer then escorted Paul and Silas from prison and asked how he could gain salvation. They replied that if he believed in the "Lord Jesus" both he and his household would be saved. They then preached to him and his household,

Held by chains, Paul and Silas are shown here in prison. This 16th-century Flemish panel is part of a window in St. Mary Magdalene Church in Mulbarton, Norfolk.

and, after the jailer had cleaned their wounds, they baptised everyone. The jailer took them to his home – probably situated next to the prison – and fed them before returning them to the jail.

The next day, when the magistrates learned that Paul and Silas were Roman citizens, they were terrified of the consequences of their illegal treatment of them – Roman law forbade flogging a Roman citizen without trial. So the magistrates ordered Paul and Silas to be freed and urged the two men to leave the town. Paul was outraged that the men who had flogged them without trial now wanted to get rid of them "on the quiet". He demanded that the officials escort him and Silas in person and in public. It was important to be seen leaving with dignity, if only to safeguard the standing of the Christians they would leave behind. Before Paul and Silas left, they visited Lydia's house to encourage the new disciples.

✝ The exorcism and the earthquake ✝

Luke's vivid account of the events at Philippi – including the conversions, exorcism and imprisonment – gives an idea of the range of people and situations Paul encountered on his mission. In Philippi alone, Paul dealt with a well-to-do female dye trader, a slave girl and a jailer. All three of them had a low societal status by virtue of their gender or work. But Paul ignored sexual and social distinctions. His aim was to bring people from all walks of life into the faith.

Some scholars question the authenticity of sections of Luke's account, especially the exorcism and the earthquake. But the idea that a possessed person could be healed by an appeal to divine authority was familiar in the ancient world. Jesus' opponents never questioned his ability to carry out exorcisms, only the authority by which he performed them.

The earthquake scenario presents other problems. Some scholars have pointed out that Luke's account resembles other escape-by-earthquake

The remains of the prison where Paul and Silas were imprisoned can still be found in present-day Philippi, Greece. Luke reported that an earthquake "shook the prison to its foundations".

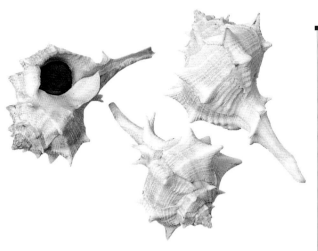

Hundreds of rock shells, or neogastropods, were crushed to produce enough purple dye to colour just one garment. Purple cloth was affordable only to the rich. As a result, Lydia was made wealthy through her purple-dye trade.

stories known in antiquity. Earthquakes were not unusual in the region, however, and it is not implausible that one occurred on the night that Paul and Silas were imprisoned.

> " *'Without trial they gave us a public flogging, though we are Roman citizens...'* "
>
> ACTS 16:37

Before leaving Philippi, with their wounds stinging but their heads held high, Paul and Silas said farewell to Lydia and the other new converts of Philippi. Although Luke does not mention the appointment of church officials, Paul referred to "elders" and "deacons" in his letter to the Philippians (1:1). Paul probably followed the pattern that he had established in the first mission: "In each of these churches they appointed elders... [Acts 14:23]". In any case, a new church was established at Philippi, and I   apparently enjoyed the friendship of its members, as his letter to them suggests: "For God will testify for me how much I long for you all with the warm longing of Christ Jesus [Philippians 1:8]." ▪

MESSAGE
— *for* —
TODAY

MANY PEOPLE TODAY, like Paul, are held as prisoners of conscience for their beliefs. Other people are imprisoned by their inflexible attitudes or physical addictions. Still others are enslaved and exploited for profit, like the possessed slave girl whom Paul liberated.

Writing to the church at Rome, Paul compared the bondage of sin from which Christ frees the believer to his own experience of being held prisoner and being miraculously set free. He went on to write that "being freed from serving sin, you took uprightness as your master [Romans 6:18]". This was a reminder that freedom runs far deeper than even the most imprisoning of circumstances. It is personal faith in Jesus that can open the door to spiritual freedom, which should be the gateway to a righteous way of life.

CONVERSIONS and RIOTS

In THESSALONICA and BEREA
ACTS 17:1–15

> ❝ 'And the Christ,' he said, 'is this Jesus
> whom I am proclaiming to you.' ❞
> ACTS 17:3

FROM PHILIPPI, Paul and his group travelled west on the Egnatian Way. Passing Amphipolis and Apollonia, they arrived at Thessalonica, the capital of Macedonia. On his arrival there, Paul "as usual" made his way to the synagogue.

For three Sabbaths Paul discussed the Gospel with the Jews to show them that Jesus' death and resurrection fulfilled the scriptures. Some Jews were convinced by Paul's arguments, as were many God-fearing Greeks and "leading women" of the city. But other Jews, who were "full of resentment" at Paul's success, decided to make trouble. Supported by a "gang from the market-place", they caused an uproar in the city, then went to the house of Jason, where the disciples were staying. The instigators' plan to drag the missionaries before the governing assembly failed, however, because they were unable to find Paul and his group. Instead, the Jews arrested Jason and some other Christians and brought them before the city magistrates.

The Jews shouted before the magistrates that the people who were causing disturbances everywhere they went – Paul and his companions – were in the city and staying with Jason. They then said that the missionaries were breaking Roman law by claiming that Jesus was a rival king of the emperor. Alarmed by this, the magistrates made "Jason and the rest give security before setting them free". They bound Jason over to dissuade Paul from preaching in the city.

When it was dark, the Thessalonian Christians sent Paul and Silas to Berea, 70 km (45 miles) to the west. Again, Paul made contact with the local synagogue. He found that the Jews in Berea were "more noble-minded than those in Thessalonica, and they welcomed the word very readily". Receptive to Paul's message, they read the scriptures every day, not just on the Sabbath, to see whether Paul was right. A large number of them became Christians, as did many "Greek women of high standing" and men.

But the scene of harmony that Luke depicts in his account did not last. When the hostile Thessalonian Jews heard that Paul was preaching in Berea, they went to that city and stirred up the people against him. While Silas and Timothy stayed behind, the local Christians arranged for Paul to go to the coast with an escort. Paul and the escort then travelled south to Athens, presumably by boat, and his escort returned to Berea to give instructions to Silas and Timothy to rejoin Paul as soon as possible.

✝ Evidence from the scriptures ✝

Luke's account of Paul's stay in Thessalonica is very brief, suggesting that Luke was not with him on that occasion. The description in Acts, however, can be supplemented by information given by Paul in his letters. Luke indicates that Paul's stay lasted at least three weeks. Paul implies that he remained in Thessalonica long enough to

require that he work "night and day" to support himself (1 Thessalonians 2:9), probably as a tent-maker, and to necessitate "gifts" from the disciples at Philippi (Philippians 4:16–17).

Paul's evangelical methods certainly included the type of sermon he delivered in the synagogue at Antioch in Pisidia (pp. 20–23). Luke wrote that Paul made use of a close analysis of the Hebrew scriptures, which were a source of inspiration that would be common to both Jews and Christians. Probably citing passages from Isaiah 53 and Psalms 2, 16 and 110, Paul argued that the scriptures pre-dicted that the Christ – the Greek word for

The structure of this synagogue in Jerusalem's old city is similar to that of the synagogues of Paul's time. The men congregate in the main section, and the women gather on a balcony above them.

"Messiah" – had to "suffer and rise from the dead". Jesus of Nazareth, he claimed, had fulfilled this role. Paul follows a similar vein in his letter to the Corinthians (1 Corinthians 15:3–8), a passage that, many scholars believe, reflects early Christian teaching. In that case, Paul was preaching orthodox Christian precepts, not following his own personal line of argument.

A Hellenistic statue, this lion sits on a pedestal near the Strimon River. Paul would have passed it as he travelled on the Egnatian Way.

The Egnatian Way, the major highway that ran from Neapolis to the Adriatic coast, is still used as a major thoroughfare today. Paul, Silas and their group travelled along this road on the way to Thessalonica.

In Berea, the local Jews initially received the missionaries' efforts sympathetically. Apparently open-minded and intellectually curious, they eagerly checked the scriptures each day to corroborate Paul's assertions. It was only when the Thessalonian Jews arrived, with their rabble-rousing tactics, that Paul was forced to leave.

✝ *The missionaries accused* ✝

Paul's methods were evidently successful, and his new converts included some of the city's "leading women" (the Greek phrase used could also mean "wives of the leading men"). In fact, the Thessalonian church was clearly supported by the city's Gentile women. But Paul's success led to trouble. Luke says that some Jews were resentful of Paul's success in attracting followers to the faith, so they stirred up opposition; but it is also possible that some of the Jews were upset because they genuinely disagreed with Paul's claims.

These hostile Jews tried to bring Paul and Silas before the demos – the popular assembly – but

they failed. Instead, they vented their anger on Jason and "some of the brothers", dragging them in front of the magistrates. Luke calls them politarchs, a term that some scholars once thought to be incorrect because it had not been found in other sources. However, inscriptions discovered in Thessalonica have now confirmed that this was the correct term for non-Roman officials in Macedonia in Paul's and Luke's time.

> " *'They have broken Caesar's edicts by claiming that there is another king, Jesus.'* "
>
> ACTS 17:7

Luke recorded in his account that the missionaries were accused of "turning the whole world upside down"; the Greek literally means "causing trouble everywhere". They were also charged with breaking "Caesar's edicts" by declaring Jesus king, making him a rival of the emperor. For Jews, the word *Christ* (which was meant as "Messiah") signified "king", a title that was often applied informally to the Roman emperors; so it would be easy for the hostile group to misrepresent the disciples' message to the authorities. At the time of Paul, Roman decrees outlawed the act of predicting a change of emperor, and it is possible that Paul's message was construed in this way. In any case, the magistrates demanded that Paul stop preaching, and they made Jason responsible for ensuring this.

Luke's account of what happened after Paul's departure is probably a simplified sketch. Details from one of Paul's letters (1 Thessalonians 3:1–6) suggest that Timothy and Silas joined him at Athens, as instructed, returned to Macedonia, and later met him in Corinth (Acts 18:5). Luke and Paul both indicate that the Gospel had spread like wildfire from Asia Minor to Macedonia; now the word of God was about to blaze its trail of salvation into one of the most illustrious cities of antiquity – Athens. ∎

MESSAGE
—for—
TODAY

ALTHOUGH CHRISTIANS *and Jews still disagree about Jesus' status, just as many of the Jews at Thessalonica disagreed with Paul, the old hostility is today being replaced in some circles by dialogue and friendship.*

Jews expected the Messiah to bring in a new era of peace and justice. They did not think of him as a divine figure, nor did they expect the Messiah to suffer or rise from the dead. In the past, Christians blamed and even persecuted Jews for not recognising Jesus as "their" Messiah. Now Christians acknowledge that Jesus did not fulfil the traditional Jewish expectations of the Messiah. In fact, the first Christians gave a new meaning to the word Messiah or Christ. Despite continuing differences, the Jewishness of Jesus links Christians closely to the Jewish people. Both long for the full coming of God's kingdom.

DEBATING
with PHILOSOPHERS

PAUL PREACHES *in* ATHENS
ACTS 17:16–34

> " *And in the marketplace he debated every day
> with anyone whom he met.* "
>
> ACTS 17:17

T ATHENS, while Paul was waiting for Silas and Timothy to join him from Macedonia, he had the chance to look around one of the great cities of the Western world. Although fallen from its former greatness of the fifth century BC, when it was renowned for its philosophers, artists, dramatists and statesmen, Athens was still the most prestigious intellectual centre of the Roman Empire. Yet everywhere Paul went, he saw statues of pagan gods, and his "whole soul was revolted" by such tangible evidence of idolatry.

As the days passed, Paul spent his time debating with the Athenian Jews and God-fearers in the city's synagogue. He then headed for the agora, or marketplace, to talk to anyone who would listen. Apparently, there were plenty of people willing to do so because, as Luke adds, listening to the latest intellectual fads was the Athenians' favourite pastime.

Among those Paul met were philosophers of the Epicurean and Stoic schools. The Epicureans, named for their founder, Epicurus (341–270 BC), believed that the gods were too remote to influence the world, and that death ended existence utterly. They stressed the importance of pleasure in life – intellectual pleasure, that is, not the sensuality often associated with them. The Stoics were named for the stoa, or colonnade, where

their founder, Zeno (335–263 BC), taught. They believed that God exists in everything – a belief called pantheism – and that people should live self-sufficient and dutiful lives.

† *An invitation to speak* †

These philosophers initially scorned Paul, calling him a *spermologos* – literally, a bird that picks up seeds – which implied that Paul collected intellectual titbits. Some probably thought that when Paul talked about "Jesus and Resurrection", he was referring to two "outlandish gods". Yet his teaching intrigued them, and they invited him to the Areopagus to explain his doctrine. The Areopagus (the Hill of Ares, or Mars Hill) was situated near the Acropolis and at one time served as the meeting place for the court, or council, of Areopagus. This group considered itself responsible for religious and educational matters; by Paul's time, it met in the Royal Portico, located in the northwest corner of the agora.

Paul complied with their request. Standing before the entire council, he began by complimenting them on their devotion to "religious" matters. He told them that as he had strolled around their sacred monuments, he had come across an altar inscribed "To an Unknown God". Referring to this altar, he continued, "In fact, the

unknown God you revere is the one I proclaim to you." He said that God, the Lord of Heaven and Earth, who had created the world, did not inhabit temples. One can imagine Paul glancing toward the magnificent Parthenon temple that crowned the Acropolis as he said this.

Nor did God want anything that humans could provide, Paul added, for it was God who gave people everything, including their life and breath. God created people from "one single principle" – a phrase that may refer to Adam, the

In a cartoon created for the Sistine Chapel, Raphael Sanzio of Urbino (1483–1520) illustrated his version of Paul preaching before a crowd of philosophers in Athens. A statue of a pagan god can be seen to the right.

first man – to live on the Earth, and he "decreed the times and limits of their habitation". Paul may have meant that God laid down the order of the seasons and the boundary between the habitable Earth and the primal waters (Genesis 1:9–10); or perhaps he was referring to different nations'

This view of the Propylaea can be seen from the Areopagus, where Paul was invited to preach. The Propylaea was the great entrance hall of the Athenian Acropolis, designed by Mnesicles in the fifth century BC.

allotted periods of ascendancy and their territorial boundaries. In either case, Paul was saying that God had ordered the universe to inspire people to seek Him out by "feeling their way toward Him".

But God was not far away, Paul stressed, for in Him "we live, and move, and exist", a phrase that was originally coined by a Cretan poet named Epimenides. Then, quoting another Greek poet, Aratus, Paul proclaimed to the council, "We are all His children." And if people are God's children, Paul argued, then it follows that idols, which consist not of flesh and blood but of metal or stone can never resemble Him.

Luke's summary of Paul's speech ends with Paul stating that God had overlooked times in the past when people were ignorant of Him. But now, with the advent of the Gospel, the situation had changed. People must repent because God had fixed a day when the world would be judged by a man "he had appointed". And God had given proof of this appointment by raising Jesus from the dead. Paul indicates that by virtue of being resurrected, Jesus acquired the authority to judge humankind – an idea that also appears in his letter to the Romans (1:4).

When the Greeks heard Paul speak of "rising from the dead", some of them could not contain their laughter. Others said that they wanted to hear more at "another time". Yet a few people were convinced, including Dionysus the Areopagite, probably a well-to-do council member, and a woman called Damaris.

✝ Wisdom for the Greeks ✝

Luke's account of Paul's speech, like his record of Paul's sermon at Lystra (pp. 26–29), gives an insight into the way Paul dealt with a pagan audience. Instead of citing the scriptures, Paul relied on "natural theology", the idea that God's existence can be inferred from the inherent order of the world and nature. While the Lystrans had been mostly uneducated people, the Athenians were intellectually sophisticated. So Paul included allusions that were calculated to whet the interest of the philosophers present. The Epicureans, for example, agreed with Paul's attitude toward pagan superstition and idol worship. And the Stoics liked the idea of an intimate connection between God and humans. But Paul went further than both their worldviews and challenged them with notions of resurrection and judgment.

> **" At this mention of rising from the dead, some of them burst out laughing... "**
> ACTS 17:32

Some scholars have questioned whether Luke's account of Paul's speech is accurate, saying that the words used are not typical of Paul. They point out that the letter of Paul that comes closest to this speech in content, Romans (1–3), differs in both tone and language. But other scholars have argued that the letter to the Romans was addressed to converted Christians, not pagan Gentiles, and that there is nothing in Acts that is inconsistent with Paul's own thought. They also think that if Luke had invented it, he would probably have emphasised the Christian content more than is evident and described a more enthusiastic response by the Greeks.

But Luke gives the impression that only a few converts were made in Athens, and none of Paul's letters mentions any church at Athens. It would appear that for most of the Greek philosophers, the Gospel was at once too radical and too simple. Paul indicates their attitude in 1 Corinthians: "While the Jews demand miracles and the Greeks look for wisdom, we are preaching a crucified Christ: to the Jews an obstacle they cannot get over, to the Gentiles foolishness...[1:22–23]." ∎

MESSAGE
—for—
TODAY

WHEN PAUL VISITED ATHENS, he found it to be a centre for philosophical debate; but he was "revolted at the sight of a city given over to idolatry" Even so, before speaking to the Athenians, he looked around. He prefaced his speech with references to an altar he had noticed, and he quoted from the Greek poets as he developed his argument for one true God and a resurrected Christ.

To communicate with others, we need to understand their interests and concerns so that we can establish a common ground — a common language, so to speak. All the more should we seek understanding when we hope to communicate a message that is of the utmost importance to us. We can earn the right to be heard by first listening, and the ability to convince others can be gained by showing a sympathy for the viewpoints of our audience.

The CITY of CORRUPTION

The DISCIPLES TURN to CORINTH

ACTS 18:1–17

> **"** *'Be fearless; speak out and*
> *do not keep silence: I am with you.'* **"**
>
> ACTS 18:9

FOLLOWING HIS MEAGRE success at Athens, Paul travelled to Corinth (p. 90), in the province of Achaea, hoping for a better response to his teaching. But the city's wealth had bred corruption by Paul's time, and the name Corinth had become a byword for immorality.

During his stay in the city, Paul met Aquila and his wife, Priscilla, Jewish refugees from Rome. They, like Paul, earned a living by making tents, and Paul moved in with them so that they could work together. He continued his missionary work, going to the synagogue every Sabbath and preaching to the local Jews and God-fearers.

Silas and Timothy arrived from Macedonia with a gift from the disciples there, perhaps a subsidy of money. Paul refers to it in 2 Corinthians: "For the brothers of Macedonia brought me as much as I needed when they came [11:9]." It enabled Paul to preach full-time and proclaim his message that "Jesus was the Christ", or Messiah – his principal theme when preaching to the Jews.

A number of Jews took offence at his words and, on one occasion, shouted insults at him. In response, Paul "took his cloak and shook it out in front of them", a gesture to show that he was breaking off relations with them. Their rejection, he said, placed responsibility for their "blood", or punishment, on themselves. Henceforth, he would devote himself to the Gentiles with a clear conscience. Paul stopped visiting the synagogue and set up an alternative centre of worship in the

house of a convert named Justus. This did not ultimately preclude some success with the Jews – in fact, the president of the synagogue, Crispus, and his household converted. Luke also says that many God-fearers were baptised into the faith.

✝ Words of encouragement ✝

At some stage, Paul may have been discouraged by his lack of progress and may have contemplated leaving the city. Luke recorded that one night Paul had a vision of the Lord, who told him to be fearless and to preach the Gospel, and assured him that He was with him and that, with so many believers in the city, no one would harm him. "So Paul stayed there," Luke says, "preaching the word of God among them for 18 months."

The situation changed, however, after a new Roman proconsul named Gallio was appointed to govern Achaea. In a "concerted attack", the Jews brought Paul before Gallio at a tribunal and accused him of "persuading people to worship God in a way that breaks the Law", that is, the Jewish Law. But Gallio dismissed their charge as a dispute over terminology, refused to pronounce judgment, and had them hustled out of court.

Immediately, Luke recorded, they turned on Sosthenes, now the synagogue's president, and "beat him in front of the tribunal". It is not clear who did the beating or why. Some scholars believe that a crowd of Gentiles was encouraged by the disdain Gallio showed toward the Jews and

One of Paul's visions is illustrated in this 16th-century painting by the Italian School. The cherubs, probably derived from Near Eastern mythology, represent in Christianity the celestial attendants of God.

vented their anti-Jewish feelings on the Jewish leader. Others think the Jews themselves attacked Sosthenes, making him a scapegoat for their failure to make a favourable impression on Gallio.

✝ The conversion of sinners ✝

Although Luke does not mention it, Paul must have been shocked by Corinth's notorious immorality. Paul himself alludes to sexual impro-prieties, for example, in 1 Corinthians (5:1–3). Nonetheless, he continued to preach, no doubt realising that the city's dens of iniquity would provide rich opportunities for evangelising. In fact, in 1 Corinthians (6:9–10), Paul mentions that some of his converts were drawn from the ranks of the city's "sexually immoral, idolaters, adulterers, the self-indulgent, sodomites, thieves, misers, drunkards, slanderers and swindlers".

Paul almost certainly owed some of his success to the individuals he befriended in Corinth, such as his fellow tentmakers, Aquila and Priscilla, who allowed Paul to reside with them. They had come to Corinth from Rome, Luke says, because of Emperor Claudius's edict expelling the Jews from the city. Contemporary Roman sources indicate that an edict to this effect was issued in AD 49 as a result of a disturbance between Christians and Jews. In fact, Aquila and Priscilla probably became Christians in Rome since Luke does not mention Paul converting or baptising them.

> ❝ *Paul devoted all his time to preaching, declaring to the Jews that Jesus was the Christ.* ❞
> ACTS 18:5

Justus allowed his house to be used as a Chris-tian meeting place. Crispus, the synagogue presi-dent whom Paul baptised himself (1 Corinthians 1:14), added his influence to the cause. Gallio, the brother of Seneca (the Roman Stoic philosopher and tutor of Emperor Nero), lent a different type of support to Paul. As proconsul of Achaea, Gallio would have governed for one year only, begin-ning on 1 July, and most scholars are certain this occurred in AD 51–52 – a rare absolute date in the chronology of Paul's history. Gallio's good charac-ter is attested to by several Roman writers. His brother Seneca said, "No man was ever as kind to

The bema of Corinth is where Gallio held his court of justice when Paul was accused of heresy by the Jews. In ancient Greece, the bema was located at the agora – the marketplace or open meeting space – in town.

A nomadic Turkish woman spins yarn outside her tent, which is similar in construction to the tents that Paul made. Paul's tents would have been made from animal skins or fabric woven from sheep's wool or goat's hair.

MESSAGE
—for—
TODAY

PRIOR TO CORINTH, Paul had responded to violent opposition – as in Iconium and Lystra – by fleeing at once to the next city. But when trouble was brewing in Corinth, he had a vision of the Lord, who promised to keep him out of harm's way: "I am with you...no one will attempt to hurt you [Acts 18:10]." So Paul stayed on for many months. He also gave up his living as a tentmaker, allowing others to provide for him so that he could concentrate on preaching.

Many people have found that when they take a risk for God's work, perhaps by braving opposition or giving up the security of a good job, God does indeed stand by them and provide for them. Like Paul, they discover the truth of God's promise, "My grace is enough for you: for power is at full stretch in weakness [2 Corinthians 12:9]."

one person as Gallio is to everyone", and this seems to have been supported by Pliny, Tacitus and Dio Cassius.

Although Gallio was new to his office and the Jews were united in their attack, he did not give in under the pressure to convict Paul. There was nothing illegal about practising a foreign cult, and Paul did not represent a threat to public morals or to the state. So Gallio acted swiftly and decisively in Paul's favour. To Luke, Gallio's behaviour showed that the impartial legal machinery of Rome could be put to the service of Christianity.

Paul ended his second missionary journey when he left Corinth with Priscilla and Aquila and sailed back to Syria via Ephesus (pp. 54–59). In Ephesus, Paul made a fleeting visit to the local synagogue before resuming his voyage to Antioch in Syria. During the journey, he landed at Caesarea and probably visited the church at Jerusalem before travelling north to Antioch. Back at Antioch, he told his brethren how the Holy Spirit had inspired him to take the "word of God" to the pagan Roman Empire. ▪

EUROPE

ILLYRICUM

ADRIATIC SEA

BLACK SEA

MACEDONIA

THRACE

Philippi
Amphipolis
Neapolis
Thessalonica
Apollonia
Berea

AEGEAN SEA

Larissa

Troas
Assos

ASIA MINOR

ASIA
Pergamum

PHRYGIA Antioch
(Pisidia)

Iconiur

LESBOS

Smyrna

PISIDIA

Lystra

CHIOS

Corinth
ACHAEA

SAMOS

Ephesus
Miletus

Derbe

PAMPHYLIA

LYCIA
Patara

TAU
MOU

COS

RHODES

CRETE

CY

MEDITERRANEAN SEA

Paul's third missionary journey
started on land when he travelled from Antioch in Syria
into Asia Minor to Ephesus. From there he went on to
Troas and journeyed through Macedonia to Corinth. He
returned through Macedonia, then sailed to Troas and on
across the Mediterranean Sea until he reached Jerusalem.

EGYPT

To EPHESUS
and
BEYOND

GALATIA

CILICIA
rsus

Antioch
(Syria)

SYRIA

PHOENICIA

Tyre
Ptolemais
Caesarea
JUDEA
Jerusalem
DEAD
SEA

100   200   300 KM

50   100   150   200 MILES

THE THIRD MISSIONARY JOURNEY

ACTS 18:23–21:16

PAUL'S THIRD JOURNEY began with a pastoral tour through Galatia and Phrygia in Asia Minor, where he consolidated the congregations already established and set up his headquarters in Ephesus for three years. Luke's account of what followed is sketchy. In 2 Corinthians 2:12, Paul states that he travelled to Troas. Luke says only that Paul made his way from Macedonia to "Greece"; he omits Paul's trip to Illyricum in the west of Greece, which Paul talks about in Romans 15:9. Paul spent three months in Corinth, where he wrote his letter to the Romans (perhaps the most important one), then returned to Macedonia. From there he sailed back to Troas and made his way along the coast of Asia Minor before crossing the Mediterranean Sea to Tyre in Syria. The mission ended in Jerusalem via Ptolemais and Caesarea.

The focus of Paul's third journey is his stay in Ephesus, where he experienced both success and opposition. Luke does not mention it, but some scholars believe that Paul was imprisoned there. At one point, Paul thought that his life was in jeopardy, possibly from ill health or persecution. Even so, Ephesus was the high point in his career. It was there that he wrote the letters of 1 Corinthians and Galatians, and many scholars think his theological development reached its peak. At the same time, as recorded in Acts (24:17) and his letters (Romans 15:26 and Galatians 2:1), Paul organised a collection of money to be taken by the representatives of the Gentile churches to the Christians in Jerusalem. He hoped this would help unite the Jewish and Gentile members of the church. ▪

The RIOT of the SILVERSMITHS

PAUL'S STAY in EPHESUS
ACTS 19:1–40

> " *The evil spirit replied, 'Jesus I recognise, and Paul I know, but who are you?'* "
> ACTS 19:15

BEFORE LEAVING EPHESUS at the end of his second missionary journey to resume his voyage to Syria, Paul said to the Ephesians, "I will come back another time, God willing [Acts 18:21]." The opportunity came during his third mission, when he stayed in the city for almost three years – the exact dates are uncertain.

Paul began his latest expedition by travelling to the churches established in Galatia and Phrygia in Asia Minor, where he encouraged the followers of the faith – many of whom were converted during his previous mission. He continued westward across Asia Minor and made his way to Ephesus (p. 90), a bustling centre of trade. This city, the largest and most important in the Roman province Asia, was a "free" city. This meant that it had its own citizen assembly – that is, Rome allowed the Ephesians to decide their own legislation. Ephesus claimed its greatest fame from the temple built for the Greek goddess Artemis (the Roman Diana), who had been amalgamated with the Ephesians' own local fertility goddess. The temple served as the centre for her cult.

While in Ephesus, Paul met a group of about 12 disciples of the Christian faith. When he asked them if they had received the Holy Spirit, they told him that they did not understand what he was referring to. They had been baptised into the faith "with John's baptism", the water baptism commanded by John the Baptist, the cousin and forerunner of Jesus.

Paul reminded them of what John himself had proclaimed about his mission. John's baptism, he said, was concerned with the repentance of sins – John had insisted that someone would follow him who would baptise "with the Holy Spirit [John 1:33]". Paul told them that this person was Jesus, and baptised them in Jesus' name then and there.

As Paul laid his hands on them, the Holy Spirit "came down on them, and they began to speak in tongues and to prophesy". The phrase *speaking in tongues* refers to the phenomenon of speaking in an ecstatic but unintelligible language inspired by the Spirit of God. Prophecy, in this context, appears to refer to the gift of proclaiming truths and predicting the future in an inspired, intelligible utterance. Paul himself discusses both of these phenomena in one of his letters [1 Corinthians 14].

† Of healings and exorcisms †

Following his normal routine, Paul set about establishing the church in Ephesus by first preaching in the local synagogue. But after three months, his Jewish audience grew ever more sceptical of his message until they openly attacked

"the Way" – the church – in public. So Paul discontinued his visits to the synagogue and arranged to hold discussions in a lecture room belonging to an Ephesian named Tyrannus, who may have been a teacher. This was clearly a happy arrangement because, Luke records, Paul stayed in Ephesus for almost three years, and the word of God radiated from the city into the towns and villages of the surrounding countryside.

The temple of Artemis at Ephesus was one of the seven wonders of the ancient world. Wilhelm von Ehrenberg's 17th-century painting shows an imaginative, though inaccurate, version of the temple.

Paul healed and exorcised numerous people through the power of God. Even articles of clothing that he had touched, including handkerchiefs and aprons, became instruments of healing.

The gateway to Curetes Street in Ephesus is just one indication of the city's size and importance. The street was home to three temples, earning the city the title Neokoros, *or temple warden.*

Luke stresses the efficacy of Paul as miracle-worker in an incident involving a group of itinerant Jewish exorcists. Wandering healers and exorcists were common in the ancient world. They travelled from one town to another, usually reciting long lists of gods whose names were thought to invoke the divine help necessary to perform a miracle. Pagans often included the different Jewish names for God in their formulas.

On this particular occasion, a group of seven Jewish exorcists, the sons of a "Jewish chief priest" named Sceva, tried to cast out evil spirits from a possessed man by invoking the name of "Jesus whose spokesman is Paul".

The evil spirit, speaking with the clairvoyance often associated with the possessed, replied that it knew Jesus and Paul but not the exorcists. Then the possessed man attacked them and ripped their clothes. As news of what had happened spread, the name of Jesus increased in prestige. Christian converts who had formerly practised magic now publicly burned their books of spells and esoteric formulas, popularly known as "Ephesian letters".

The value of these books, Luke relates, was 50,000 pieces of silver (one piece of silver was the typical wage for one working day), making their destruction a considerable financial sacrifice.

With the church established in Ephesus, Paul planned to visit Macedonia and Achaea, in part to collect money for the church at Jerusalem, before returning to Jerusalem. Luke omits this, but Paul mentions it in 1 Corinthians: "Do not delay the collection till I arrive…I will send to Jerusalem…those people you approve of to deliver your gift [16:2–3]."

Luke also says it was at this moment that Paul decided to go to Rome – the wording of the original Greek text suggests that it was his destiny to do so. His purpose was not to establish a church – one already existed there by this time – but, as Paul mentions in his letter to the Romans, to impart "some spiritual gift [1:11]".

✝ The silversmiths' challenge ✝

Paul sent the disciples Timothy and Erastus to Macedonia, intending to join them later on. At the time, while still in Ephesus, a dramatic event occurred that nearly imperilled Paul's life. It began with the silversmiths of the city, who made a profitable living selling silver models of the temple of Artemis (bought in the same manner that tourists' trinkets are today). The silversmiths' leader, Demetrius, called a meeting in which he convinced his fellow craftsmen that Paul and his vehement message of anti-idolatry threatened their livelihood and diminished the prestige of their goddess Artemis.

Roused to anger by Demetrius's words, the silversmiths began to shout a rallying cry supporting their goddess. Soon, this cry had spread and set the city in an uproar. A mob seized two of Paul's companions, Gaius and Aristarchus, and dragged them off to the city's great open-air theatre. They hoped to convene an assembly of citizens who could persuade the Ephesian city officials to act against the missionaries. Although

Paul tried to intervene, his friends – including some high-ranking provincial officials – restrained him, fearing for his safety.

> ❝ *This man Paul has persuaded and converted a great number of people with his argument that gods made by hand are not gods at all.* ❞
> ACTS 19:26

Meanwhile, the theatre became a scene of chaos, with people "shouting different things" and, in some cases, not knowing why they were even there. A Jew named Alexander attempted to address the mob, but he was shouted down with "Great is Artemis of the Ephesians!" These chants continued for two hours. Eventually, the "town

Paul healing a man is shown in this 17th-century etching by Matthäus Merian. Paul performed numerous healings in Ephesus, which attracted many converts.

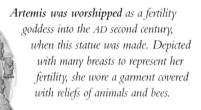

Artemis was worshipped as a fertility goddess into the AD second century, when this statue was made. Depicted with many breasts to represent her fertility, she wore a garment covered with reliefs of animals and bees.

clerk", the city's main magistrate, arrived to restore order. Addressing the riotous crowd, he assured them that the city's fame as the guardian of Artemis's temple was safe. The clerk pointed out that the Christians were not guilty of any blasphemy against the goddess, but if Demetrius and his colleagues had a complaint, there were legal procedures they could follow. More to the point, he warned them, there could be serious repercussions from the Roman authorities if word reached them that the Ephesians had been rioting. The clerk's calm and rational words dispelled the mob's hysteria, and he was finally able to dismiss the assembled throng from the theatre.

✝ The lessons taught ✝

Luke's account of Paul's stay in Ephesus records several incidents that illustrate different aspects of Paul's mission there: the nature of Christian baptism; the power of Jesus' name in healings; the growth of the church and its threat to paganism; and the legality of the missionaries' procedures.

But, as is clear from Paul's letters, Luke does not give all the details. In 1 Corinthians, a letter Paul may have written from Ephesus, he refers to fighting "wild animals" in the city (15:32) – a metaphor for an incident of human opposition

that Luke does not report. In 2 Corinthians (11:23–26), Paul mentions afflictions that may refer to his stay there. Some scholars also speculate that Paul may have been imprisoned in the city (Paul mentions imprisonment in Colossians 4:3).

> ❝ *These men… are not guilty of any sacrilege or blasphemy against our goddess.* ❞
> ACTS 19:37

One of the most memorable incidents that Luke describes in Acts is the hostile reaction that Paul received from the Ephesian silversmiths, who feared the detrimental effect Paul's preaching

would have on their pagan religion and, with it, their livelihood. The reaction was similar to the one Paul had provoked at Philippi (pp. 36–39) when he exorcised the possessed slave girl. By including this incident, Luke demonstrates that those who had official authority opposed unreasonable action against the Christians. This was most likely because the Christian faithful, as Luke insisted, did not pose a threat to the Roman state and had as much legal right to live and worship in the empire as the other religions and sects of its pluralistic society. ▪

The theatre at Ephesus measures about 150 m (500 feet) in diameter and, in Paul's time, held as many as 25,000 people. It was here that the silversmiths rioted.

MESSAGE
—for—
TODAY

THE EPHESIAN SILVERSMITHS were justifiably worried that their livelihood would be destroyed if the citizens of Ephesus listened to Paul and gave up worshipping the goddess Artemis. But instead of reasoning with Paul, they incited a mob against him.

People who sense that their livelihood is threatened, even for the good of the community, may react with irrational or violent opposition. At the heart of such a reaction is fear, and it stands in contrast to a response of faith. Those who believed Paul's word could face the prospect of change with the assurance that God would provide for their needs. When we encounter change that makes us angry, we should stop and ask ourselves why. Life involves constant change and growth, and our anger may hide a reluctance to listen to the voice of conscience and an underlying lack of faith in God's provision.

A RAISING *from the* DEAD

From EPHESUS *to* TROAS

ACTS 20:1–12

" Paul went down and stooped to clasp the boy to him, saying, 'There is no need to worry, there is still life in him.' "

ACTS 20:10

A FTER THE RIOT in Ephesus, Paul moved on, partly to help resolve strife that had been reported within the church at Corinth and partly to raise money for the brethren at Jerusalem. Luke compresses the events of the ensuing journey, but Paul's letters, 2 Corinthians and Romans, provide additional facts. Paul first went to Troas, then crossed into Europe, probably staying at Philippi. Luke simply says that from Macedonia Paul went to "Greece", where Corinth was situated.

After three months in Corinth, Paul made plans to take the funds he had collected to Jerusalem. But "a plot organised against him by the Jews" – Luke gives no details – forced him to return to Macedonia. Some of Paul's companions went on to Troas, where they awaited the arrival of Paul and the others from Philippi after the Jewish Passover. Paul's group probably included Luke – at this point, he reintroduces the "we" and "us" into Acts (20:5–6; pp. 34–35).

At Troas, the day before he was due to leave, the Christians met in the home of a local disciple

The Last Supper in this Byzantine fresco is thought to be representative of the "breaking of bread" of the Eucharist in Paul's time. The windows in the buildings are similar in style to the one that Eutychus fell from.

for the "breaking of bread" – the term Luke uses to refer to the ritual meal of the Eucharist, or Mass, which commemorates the Last Supper of Jesus. The Troas brethren filled the meeting room on the third floor, and Paul spoke until midnight.

A young man named Eutychus, who was sitting on the sill of an open window, succumbed to sleep and fell to the ground below. The disciples rushed to see if he had survived; Luke says, "He was picked up dead." Paul, however, clasped Eutychus to him and pronounced him alive. Paul returned to the meeting room, "broke the bread and ate", and carried on preaching until dawn. Luke adds that the boy was taken away alive.

† Celebrating the Eucharist †

The story of Eutychus gives us insight into an early church meeting. Part of its purpose was to celebrate the Eucharist, which Paul refers to in 1 Corinthians 10:16. This ritual meal may have been combined with the eating of the Agape, or Love feast – a meal that the participants contributed to and ate in Christian fellowship, a sort of precursor to the modern "potluck" supper.

The meeting was probably held in a tenement building. In Roman-built cities, the structures rose up to 10 storeys high. The windows reached almost to the floor and had no glass. Eutychus probably fell asleep from fatigue and the stuffy atmosphere created by a packed audience and the burning oil lamps that Luke mentions.

Eutychus was apparently killed by the fall. Some scholars believe that Paul's remark "there is still life in him" indicates that the boy was unconscious. Luke, however, clearly states that the boy was dead (20:9) and that he was taken away alive (20:12). Luke wanted to make it clear to his readers that Paul, working with the power of God, should be regarded as a miracle-worker on the same level as Peter (Acts 9:36–43). It is also significant that the event took place at the time of Passover, when, a number of years earlier, Jesus had died and risen from the dead. ▪

MESSAGE
— for —
TODAY

PAUL'S ENERGY must have been astounding. On the day before he left Troas, Paul preached a sermon until the middle of the night, brought Eutychus back to life, broke bread, then carried on talking until he left at daybreak. Such a punishing schedule was not unusual for him, because, as he wrote to the Corinthians, "I am under compulsion" to preach the Gospel and "I should be in trouble if I failed to do it [1 Corinthians 9:16]."

If we believe, like Paul, that Christ offers individuals a new life connected to God, we too will be "ambassadors of Christ", urging people to find peace with God. The blame for the church's failure to transform society can be laid in part at the feet of apathetic Christians. As the novelist and poet G.K. Chesterton said, "The Christian ideal has not been tried and found wanting. It has been found difficult, and left untried."

A FOND FAREWELL

PAUL SAYS GOODBYE *in* MILETUS
ACTS 20:13–38

"'I have not hesitated to do anything that would be helpful to you; I have preached to you and instructed you both in public and in your homes...' "
ACTS 20:20

FTER PAUL LEFT TROAS, where the Christian community was "greatly encouraged" by his presence and his raising Eutychus from the dead, he set off by road to the town of Assos, 30 km (20 miles) to the south. There, he joined Luke and the rest of his party, who had taken a longer but less arduous journey by sea, and continued on the southerly course between the coast of Asia Minor and the islands of Lesbos, Chios and Samos. Paul's group anchored at Miletus (p. 91), a city 50 km (30 miles) south of Ephesus. Paul was eager to reach Jerusalem for the festival of the Pentecost, so he did not travel to Ephesus. Instead, he sent a message to the elders of the Ephesian church, asking them to meet him at Miletus.

When the Ephesians arrived, Paul spoke to them at length. His speech, the only one in Acts in which he addresses a purely Christian audience, conveys his passionate care for those with whom he had spent almost three years. Luke may recount the speech with particular vividness because he witnessed it.

Some scholars, however, have questioned whether the speech is faithful to Paul's original, pointing out that the language used is more typical of Luke. They attribute the apologetic tone that Paul uses to Luke, who may have written Acts after Paul's death to defend Paul from his contemporary critics. They also emphasise the similarity of this address to other "farewell" speeches in the Bible – including Jesus' farewell discourse to his disciples (John 13–16). In these speeches, the speaker warns his listeners of future trials and dangers and presents himself as a model for their behaviour.

Other scholars have shown that the content, if not the language, of the speech is consistent with Paul's thoughts and attitude and that there are a number of significant words and phrases in the speech that Paul used in his letters. Furthermore, Paul could certainly have risen to his own defence if attacks were made against him – 2 Corinthians 10–13 indicates that Paul had become used to these. In any case, Paul knew that critics of his message from both within and without the church would in all likelihood appear some time after his departure from Asia Minor. His speech may have been intended to preempt an attack on his message of salvation.

+ *The parting speech* +

Paul began his address by reminding the elders of how he had "served the Lord in all humility". In his letters, Paul speaks of being a "servant" and extols the virtue of humility (for example, in both Romans 1:1 and 2 Corinthians 11:23). He

also alluded to the "sorrows and trials" that arose from plots hatched by some of the Ephesian Jews, incidents that were omitted from Luke's account. Paul stressed how he had preached and taught the Gospel publicly and privately, to both "Jews and Greeks", a phrase Paul often used in his letters.

Describing himself as "in captivity to the Spirit", or constrained to follow God's guiding spirit, Paul informed the elders that he was on his way to Jerusalem. He did not know what fate awaited him there, he said, but indicated that

Paul taking his leave from his followers is shown in a 19th-century engraving by Julius Schnorr von Carolsfeld. Paul warned the elders of the church of Ephesus to be vigilant and persevering in their faith.

persecution and imprisonment were distinct possibilities, since the Holy Spirit had previously warned him of such treatment in other towns. Paul emphasised that whatever lay in store for him, he did not value his own life. What mattered most was the successful completion of his mission:

"to bear witness to the good news of God's grace". He then told the Ephesian elders that they would probably never see him again. He could say with a clear conscience, however, that he had done everything to proclaim to them the will of God in its entirety.

✝ The need for vigilance ✝

In the second half of his speech, Paul warned the elders to be on guard both for themselves and for their "flock", a familiar biblical image also used by Jesus (Luke 12:32; John 10:1–30). They should also care for the "church of God" – an expression Paul liked to use in his letters (for example, 1 Corinthians 1:2) – and watch out for opponents who would attack the faithful. Paul was probably referring to heretical teachers and may have had in mind an incident that occurred at Corinth. In 2 Corinthians 10–13, Paul wrote

The Miletus theatre is an indication of the status and size of the city. Miletus had commercial importance and was favoured by the Roman emperors Augustus and Trajan. Its harbours eventually silted up, leading to its decline.

that after he had departed from the city, people preaching "another Gospel" came to Corinth and led the faithful astray.

> ❝ *I know quite well that when I have gone fierce wolves will invade you and will have no mercy on the flock.* ❞
> ACTS 20:29

The Ephesians, Paul said, must also be wary of disciples from their midst, who would attract followers with a distorted version of the Gospel. They should be as vigilant and persevering in their faith as he had been while he was among them. He then commended them to God and to "the word of His grace" – the free, unearned favour of God – which, he said, had the power to build them up and ensure their share in the blessings of God's people. In other words, Paul was handing over to them the spiritual responsibility for the Ephesian church.

*The **Maeander River** in Miletus, Turkey, was used to transport both people and goods through the region. The Ephesians would have found travel to the city easy.*

Paul finished his address by citing himself as a model of proper conduct. He had not asked for financial assistance or clothing but earned money through his trade (as a tentmaker, pp. 48–51) to support himself and his companions. They should exert themselves in a similar way, so that they would have enough to help weaker Christians. To support this idea, Paul quoted Jesus as saying, "There is more happiness in giving than in receiving", words that are not recorded in the Gospels.

After Paul stopped speaking, he and the Ephesian elders prayed together, kneeling on the ground – the usual posture for prayer was standing, but on special occasions, people knelt down. Afterward, affected by his words, the tearful elders embraced and kissed him. They then accompanied Paul to the ship that would take him to Syria, Jerusalem and an uncertain fate. Some scholars have pointed out a parallel between Jesus making his way to Jerusalem at the end of his ministry, knowing that he was going to die, and Paul heading toward the same city, anticipating that imprisonment, or a worse fate, awaited him.

MESSAGE
—for—
TODAY

THERE IS GREAT SATISFACTION in a job well done, as Paul must have felt. When saying farewell to the Ephesians, he could truthfully say, "I have without faltering put before you the whole of God's purpose [Acts 20:27]". So, too, for doctors or teachers, the sense that they have done all they can for their patients or pupils is its own reward.

Paul's aim was to do the work that God had given him. He had no interest in material reward or in other people's good opinions of him. In his life, Paul exemplified the words of Jesus, that it is better to give than to receive, by giving of himself to spread the Gospel.

Any work that is a service to others requires the dedication that Paul embodied. If we see our work as entrusted to us by God, then whatever the hardships, we will want to do it to the best of our ability, regardless of any incidental personal gain.

PROPHETIC WARNINGS

PAUL *in* TYRE *and* CAESAREA

ACTS 21:1–16

" Speaking in the Spirit, they kept telling Paul
not to go on to Jerusalem. "

ACTS 21:4

FOLLOWING THEIR FAREWELL to the Christian elders of Ephesus, Paul and his party "tore themselves away" and set sail for Syria and the last lap of the third journey. They continued their course along the coast of Asia Minor, stopping en route at ports on the mainland and various islands, including Cos and Rhodes. At Patara, a major city of Lycia in southeastern Asia Minor, they changed ships, either because it was their vessel's final destination or because the ship was not suited for the 650-km (400-mile) haul they were about to make across the Mediterranean Sea.

Embarking again, this time on a cargo vessel, Paul and his group passed Cyprus and, after about five days, stopped at Tyre (p. 91). In Tyre, the chief town of Phoenicia in Syria, Paul visited the local church, which was probably founded by Christians fleeing Jerusalem after Stephen's martyrdom (Acts 8). Some of the Tyrian faithful, who evidently had the power of prophecy, foresaw the troubles that lay ahead for Paul at Jerusalem and urged him not to go there.

Paul made it clear, however, that he would not be deflected from his course. When his ship was ready to depart, he and his companions set off to the harbour. In a small but vivid detail that suggests that he may have witnessed the scenario, Luke says that Paul was escorted to his ship by a group of Tyrian women and children. When they all reached the "beach" – the built-up sandbanks bordering the causeway, or mole – they knelt down and prayed together before saying their goodbyes, a scene reminiscent of Paul's departure from Miletus (pp. 62–65).

† A warning in Caesarea †

From Tyre, the ship sailed 45 km (27 miles) south to Ptolemais (present-day Akko), a thriving Roman colony with the best anchorage in the area. Paul stayed there for one night – just long enough to meet the local Christians. The following day they reached Caesarea, most likely by the 50-km (32-mile) sea route instead of the 65-km (40-mile) journey by land, although Luke does not specify. Caesarea was the capital of the Roman province of Judea.

Among the city's disciples was Philip "the evangelist", who was "filled with the Spirit [Acts 6:3]". He was one of the seven Greek-speaking Jewish Christians who had been chosen by the 12 apostles to relieve them of the duty of administering the church's funds and resources (Acts 6:1–6). He had also preached the Gospel in Samaria, where he gained a reputation as a healer (Acts 8:5–8), and had converted an influential eunuch from the Ethiopian royal court (Acts 8:26–40).

At the time of Paul's visit, Philip apparently resided in Caesarea with his four unmarried daughters. Luke states that these women were prophets. Although he does not elaborate, he does illustrate that the gift of Christian prophecy was given freely to both men and women, a fact

that was also mentioned by Paul in one of his letters (1 Corinthians 11:5).

Luke's brief mention of these prophets is quickly followed by his account of an incident that involved a seer. Several days after they had arrived at Philip's home, Paul and his party were visited by a prophet named Agabus from Judea. Agabus had met Paul once before in Antioch; at the time, the prophet had correctly predicted that a severe famine would sweep through the empire (Acts 11:27–28). Now, in a dramatic symbolic action, Agabus "took Paul's belt and tied up his

The port of Tyre, *where Paul stayed at the end of his journey, is depicted in an engraving by W.M. Bartlett. Tyre was built on a small island joined to the mainland by an artificial causeway.*

own feet and hands", saying that the Holy Spirit had told him that the owner of the belt would be bound by the Jews in Jerusalem and handed over to the Gentiles.

Alarmed by this pronouncement, Paul's companions urged him not to proceed to Jerusalem. But their pleas did not deter Paul, who told them

A carving of a Palmyrene ship shows a typical form of transport used in Paul's time. Indeed, Paul himself may have embarked on such a vessel during his journeys.

The port of Caesarea was one of Paul's final stopping places on his way to Jerusalem at the end of his third missionary journey.

that he was prepared not only to be imprisoned in Jerusalem but also to die there. The disciples finally desisted and acknowledged that God's will had to take its course. Accordingly, they went with him to Jerusalem, accompanied by some of the Christians of Caesarea, who guided Paul to the house of a Cypriot named Mnason. The stage was now set for Paul's final confrontation with his Jewish enemies.

✝ A sense of foreboding ✝

The topographical details that Luke supplies for the last part of the third missionary journey from Miletus to Jerusalem, along with Luke's continued use of "we" (pp. 34–35), provide evidence that Luke was one of Paul's companions. Throughout the narrative, Luke gives the impression that almost everywhere Paul and his party went, they found enclaves of Christians on whom they could rely for hospitality. At the same time, Luke skilfully conveys a sense of foreboding

about the end of the mission. Paul's previous experiences, along with the prophecies of the Tyrian Christians and Agabus, made a confrontation on his return to Jerusalem seem inevitable. Even the mention of the daughters of Philip adds to the menacing atmosphere.

Agabus himself prophesied with actions and words reminiscent of some of the Old Testament prophets. In 1 Kings 11:27–39, for example, the prophet Ahijah accosted Jeroboam, the future king of Israel, and tore his new cloak into 12 strips to represent the imminent schism in King Solomon's kingdom and the 12 tribes of Israel. Here, Agabus took Paul's belt – a long strip of cloth wound around his waist – and tied his own hands and feet to show what would happen to Paul in Jerusalem.

> " 'The man to whom this girdle belongs will be tied up like this by the Jews in Jerusalem and handed over to the Gentiles.' "
>
> ACTS 21:11

As some scholars have pointed out, Agabus's prophecy was not strictly accurate. Although the Jews did capture Paul, the Romans actually rescued him from their clutches and kept him in prison partly for his own safety. Agabus's words, however, broadly convey the sense of Paul's fate, and they also draw a parallel with the fate of Jesus, who was handed over to the Romans by the Jews.

Paul's companions, after hearing Agabus's prophecy, tried to hold Paul back from Jerusalem. But Paul showed that he was committed to complete obedience to the will of God. If his friends had entertained any hope of his avoiding Jerusalem, it was definitely quashed when Paul insisted that he was ready to give his life there – if that was the price of preaching in "the name of the Lord Jesus". ▪

MESSAGE
—for—
TODAY

A GAPING CHASM exists between the fatalism expressed in the popular phrase "Whatever will be, will be" and the trusting faith inherent in the phrase "The Lord's will be done". Paul insisted on going to Jerusalem, despite the dire prophecy of Agabus and the entreaties of his companions. Paul was willing to face martyrdom, if that was God's will, because he had steadfast faith in God.

Life often involves risk, and sometimes the most meaningful actions and events of our lives are also the riskiest. When we care for someone, it is our duty to encourage the person to take the right action, even in the face of danger and potential loss. People of faith can be confident that God will protect them so that they can readily accept the Lord's will. As a result, they face the future unafraid.

EUROPE

ITALY

ADRIATIC
SEA

THRACE

Rome
Three Taverns
Forum of Appius

MACEDONIA

ASIA

Puteoli

AEGEAN
SEA

Rhegium

PAMP

LYCIA
Myra

Syracuse

Cnidus

MALTA

Phoenix
Fair Havens

CRETE
Lasea

MEDITERRANEAN S

Paul's journey to Rome
begin after his return to Jerusalem.
Taken by the Roman soldiers first to
Caesarea, he then travelled to Rome.
The voyage involved three different
ships and a shipwreck off Malta.

EGYPT

| 0 | 100 | 200 | 300 | 400 | 500 KM |

| 0 | 100 | 200 | 300 MILES |

To the
HEART of the
EMPIRE

BLACK SEA

ASIA MINOR

GALATIA

CAPPADOCIA

CILICIA

SYRIA

Sidon

JUDEA
Caesarea
Antipatris
Jerusalem

THE VOYAGE TO ROME

ACTS 21:17–28:31

L UKE'S ACCOUNT OF PAUL'S trials in Jerusalem and Caesarea and his voyage to Rome take up a quarter of Acts, which shows the importance he placed on these events. Luke was eager to portray Paul not only as an evangelist and founder of churches but also as a witness on trial for his faith in Jesus Christ.

At Jerusalem, Paul was accused by "Jews of Asia" of breaking the Law and was arrested by the Romans. They transferred him to Caesarea, where he appeared before Felix and, later, Festus, both Roman governors, as well as King Agrippa II. To avoid being tried in Jerusalem, and to take the Gospel to Rome, Paul claimed his right as a Roman citizen to be tried before the emperor. Once in Rome, he was confined to house arrest for two years.

Luke ends Acts abruptly, without saying whether Paul was tried before Caesar or what happened to him afterward, perhaps because his interest was in how the Gospel arrived at Rome. There is some speculation about what happened to Paul. One Christian tradition, formulated in the second century, claims that Paul left Rome, made a missionary journey to Spain, then returned to Rome. What is virtually certain is that Paul was executed by the Romans, perhaps during Emperor Nero's persecution of Christians after the great fire of Rome in AD 64. The fourth-century historian Eusebius wrote, "Nero was the first to be proclaimed an opponent of God, appearing for the slaughter of the apostles. History relates that Paul was beheaded, actually in Rome, during his reign…" ▪

RESCUED *by the* ROMANS

The CONSPIRACY *of the* JEWS AGAINST PAUL
ACTS 21:17–23:35

« 'This is the man who preaches to everyone everywhere against our people…' »
ACTS 21:28

I N JERUSALEM, Paul was greeted by James, Jesus' brother, and other elders of the church. They told him that many Jewish Christians in the city were upset by rumours that he was urging Jews to disregard the Law. To show that he was a faithful Jew, they suggested that he pay the expenses for four men to take the Nazirite vow, an expensive Jewish rite that lasted seven days and involved the cutting of hair and the making of sacrifices.

The next day, Paul accompanied the four men to the temple and took the purification rite himself. But at the end of the seven-day period, Jews saw Paul in the temple and accused him of preaching against Judaism and bringing Gentiles into the temple, an act that was strictly forbidden.

A mob formed, seized Paul, and began to beat him. When news of the uproar reached the Roman tribune, or commander, at the Antonia Fortress, he rescued Paul from the crowd, put him in chains, and marched him off to the fortress. Apparently, the commander mistook Paul for a notorious Egyptian bandit. Before he was taken inside, however, Paul impressed the tribune by speaking in Greek and told him that he was a Jew from Tarsus. When he asked to address the crowd, the tribune consented.

Paul began to speak to the crowd in their native Aramaic language. He outlined his credentials as a loyal Jew, describing his early life in Tarsus, his education in Jerusalem, and his anti-Christian fervour. He then spoke of his conversion. His account is similar to Luke's version (pp. 10–13), with one difference – on his return to Jerusalem, Paul said he received another vision of Christ, who told him to flee the city and preach to the Gentiles.

† A meeting of the Sanhedrin †

At the mention of Gentiles, the crowd erupted, shouting, "He is not fit to live!" The tribune took Paul inside and ordered him to be interrogated "under the lash". But before they could flog him, Paul revealed that he was a Roman citizen and legally immune from being scourged. When the tribune heard this, he feared he might be punished for his actions. The next day, he called a meeting of the Sanhedrin, the council of Jewish elders, and brought Paul along to hear what charges were being levelled against him.

Facing the assembled Sanhedrin, Paul realised that his best chance was to create dissent among the two rival groups that made up its members. These were the Sadducees, the priestly aristocrats who did not believe in the resurrection of the dead, and the Pharisees, devout Jews who believed in life after death. Paul declared that he was a Pharisee and was being tried for believing in the resurrection of the dead. At this, the factions began arguing, with some of the Pharisees supporting Paul. As the dispute intensified, the Roman tribune took Paul away to the fortress. That night, Paul received a vision of Christ, who told him he must bear witness for Him in Rome.

Paul is shown confounding *two Jewish elders, in this 12th-century painting in the Palatine Chapel in Palermo, Italy. The Roman soldier in the background is allowing the discussion to take place.*

*The **Antonia Fortress**, shown in this replica, is where the tribune ordered Paul to be taken. The original was built on rock, 24 m (80 feet) high, near Herod's temple.*

Meanwhile, a number of Jews vowed to kill Paul and plotted to ambush him. But Paul's nephew heard of the plot and informed the tribune, who decided to send Paul to Caesarea to his superior, Felix, the procurator of Judea. He sent Paul by night with an armed escort and a letter to Felix.

✝ Paul: a loyal Jew? ✝

Luke's account of Paul's escape from the mob and appearance before the Sanhedrin includes the warnings that Paul received about travelling to Jerusalem. His welcome by the Jerusalem brethren was tempered by the news that many Jewish Christians suspected that he was antagonistic to their Jewish rituals.

There is no evidence that the charge against Paul – that he urged Jews to abandon circumcision – was true. In fact, Paul had Timothy circumcised in Galatia (pp. 32–35). He also showed his concern for the Law by paying the expenses of the four men and undergoing purification himself. Athough some scholars believe that Luke invented this event to make Paul appear to be a loyal Jew, Paul's action was not inconsistent with his readiness to make a conciliatory gesture, as indicated in 1 Corinthians: "To the Jews I made myself as a Jew, to win the Jews [9:20]."

> **❝ The Lord appeared to him and said, 'Courage! You have borne witness for me ...' ❞**
> ACTS 23:11

The troubles that arose came not from Jewish Christians but from Jews from Asia, who accused Paul of taking Gentiles into the prohibited parts of the temple. Given his respect for Judaism, Paul would not have been so foolish. Nevertheless, a riot ensued, which led to Paul's arrest and his address to the mob – the first of three speeches in the last part of Acts (the two others are in 24:10–21 and 26:2–23) in which he defended himself. In this speech, he tried to convince the crowd that although he was a Christian, he was still a Jew.

The Roman tribune was puzzled by Paul and hoped that the Sanhedrin would explain Paul's crimes. But the argument between the Pharisees and the Sadducees prevented this from happening. When Paul spoke of the Resurrection, he was trying to show that in this regard Christianity was not incompatible with Pharisaic Judaism.

Paul's destiny was reaffirmed by his vision of Christ, and the Jews' vow to kill him unwittingly helped to fulfil it. The tribune realised that Paul's case was too complex and dangerous for him. Paul would have to go to the procurator. The tribune's letter, in which he gives his name as Claudius Lysias, may be Luke's guess at what the officer would have written. Lysias stated that Paul's alleged crime concerned the Law – there was no charge deserving imprisonment. Luke wanted to stress Paul's innocence of any political offence.

In Caesarea, Felix ascertained that Paul was from Cilicia but confirmed that he himself would try his case as soon as Paul's accusers – who had been notified by Lysias – arrived from Jerusalem. Until then, Paul was locked up in the old palace of Herod the Great, the procurator's residence. ■

A Roman horseman holding a spear is carved into this AD 70 stone funerary column. The Roman cavalry, among others, helped to bring Paul safely to Caesarea.

MESSAGE
—for—
TODAY

PAUL OPPOSED THE demands of some of the Jewish faithful, who thought that any Gentile believer had to be circumcised. The leaders of the church in Jerusalem backed Paul, only requiring Gentile believers to comply with parts of the Law (p. 31). But rumours persisted that Paul no longer kept to the Law. The Jerusalem church, whose members observed the Jewish Law, wanted Paul to put an end to the stories.

The early church quarrelled over God's different requirements for Jewish and Gentile believers. God treats people as individuals, but people tend to treat those who differ from themselves with suspicion and fear. As Paul demonstrated, however, we should obey God's will in our daily life without condemning others who express their discipleship differently. In this way, we help to bring God's love to the world.

The APPEAL to CAESAR

PAUL'S CAPTIVITY at CAESAREA
ACTS 24–26

" 'What I do admit to you is this: it is according to the Way, which they describe as a sect, that I worship the God of my ancestors...' "

ACTS 24:14

FIVE DAYS AFTER Paul had been confined by the Roman procurator at Caesarea, the Jewish high priest, Ananias, and other Jewish elders arrived from Jerusalem with the lawyer Tertullus to state their case against Paul. When the prisoner was summoned, Tertullus began the case by accusing Paul of causing trouble among Jewish communities abroad, of leading the "Nazarene sect" and of trying to profane the temple.

With the same courtesy to the procurator Felix that Tertullus had shown, Paul denied the charges. He admitted following the Christian faith, insisting that it was not a sect of Judaism, as Tertullus suggested, but a fulfilment of the Jewish religion, and that his belief in the Resurrection was the same as that of the Pharisees. Paul told Felix that he had come to Jerusalem to bring "relief money" to the church and that his visit to the temple had not caused a disturbance until the "Jews of Asia" had created trouble for him. Then he requested that his accusers state their charges.

At this point, Felix adjourned the case until the arrival of Lysias, the Roman tribune, and Paul was taken away into custody. But the procurator had been struck by Paul's words, and a few days later, he questioned Paul privately about his faith. As soon as Paul began to speak of "uprightness" and "the coming Judgment", however, Felix's spirit of inquiry left and he dismissed Paul.

For two years, until the end of his procuratorship, Felix kept Paul in custody, summoning him often in the hope of extracting a bribe. When Felix was replaced by Porcius Festus, the Jews petitioned the new official to send Paul to Jerusalem because they planned to ambush him en route.

+ Paul states his position +

Festus insisted that if the Jews had charges to bring against Paul they would have to do so in Caesarea. They agreed, and once again Paul stood trial. The Jews, Luke says, made "many serious accusations" that they could not substantiate, and Paul rebuffed them with one statement: "I have committed no offence whatever against either Jewish Law, or the temple, or Caesar." Festus wanted to "gain favour with the Jews", so he asked Paul if he would be tried at Jerusalem. Fearing an unfair trial, Paul "appealed to Caesar", exercising his legal right as a Roman citizen to have his case tried before the emperor in Rome.

Before Paul's departure, Luke describes the visit to Festus by Agrippa II, a local Roman-backed king, and his sister Bernice. Agrippa asked to see Paul. Festus agreed, hoping that Agrippa might explain the Jews' charges against Paul.

Paul was summoned to defend himself yet again. Addressing Agrippa, Festus and other "city notables", he told how he had been raised as a Pharisee and put on trial for his belief that, through Jesus, God had fulfilled His promise to His people. Paul explained how he had persecuted the Christians, then he described his

conversion (pp. 10–13). He went on to tell how he preached the Gospel to both Jews and Gentiles, testifying that Christ had risen from the dead, as the Jewish prophets had predicted.

Paul, bound in chains, makes his appeal of innocence before Festus, in this 19th-century stained-glass panel in Lincoln Cathedral. The purple colour of Festus's robe indicates his high rank.

Festus suddenly shouted that Paul had lost his mind. Paul turned to Agrippa for support, and the king joked that Paul had nearly converted him. Paul replied that he wished everyone present would turn to the faith. At this, Agrippa called a halt to the interview by rising to his feet. He and Festus agreed that Paul did not deserve death or imprisonment, and Agrippa added that but for Paul's appeal to Caesar, he could have been set free.

† Felix and Festus †

Paul's two-year imprisonment in Caesarea was the next stepping-stone along the path that would take him to Rome. During this time, he had to defend himself and the Gospel before two

Gold jewellery found in a first-century Roman grave in Zara, Croatia, gives an idea of how a woman of high standing would have been adorned. Bernice would have worn similar exquisite trinkets when she visited Festus with her brother King Agrippa II.

A stone relief shows Paul being escorted by the Romans. It can be found on a fourth-century Roman sarcophagus for the prefect (a governor or magistrate) Junius Bassus in St. Peter's Church, Rome.

Roman governors and a local king. Luke's sketch of Felix – including his desire to be bribed and to gain favour with the Jews by not releasing Paul from prison – agrees with the Roman historian Tacitus's opinion that Felix "exercised the power of a king with the disposition of a slave".

> **" 'You have appealed to Caesar; to Caesar you shall go.' "**
> ACTS 25:12

Little is known of Porcius Festus, but according to the Jewish historian Josephus, he was a more humane governor than his predecessor. Like Felix, however, Festus was anxious to gain the Jews' favour. It is for this reason, Luke says, that he suggested that Paul accept a trial in Jerusalem. Paul could not rely on a fair trial in that city, or even be sure of arriving there in one piece. So he made the momentous decision to appeal to Caesar, setting in motion the legal machinery that would take him to Rome.

Festus agreed to Paul's demand, knowing that he would have to explain Paul's case to the emperor. He also knew that Paul's alleged crimes were wrapped up with his belief in "a dead man called Jesus", but he still could not ascertain exactly what Paul was being accused of. Even Agrippa, a man who was familiar with Jewish history, was unable to enlighten him. Luke gives the impression that in the eyes of Agrippa and the highest-ranking Roman official in Judea, Paul had said and done nothing treasonous against the state.

Agrippa's remark to Festus that Paul could be set free but for his appeal to Caesar was not strictly true; Festus could legally have acquitted Paul. But to do so would have undermined the appeal procedure and offended the emperor – a risk no ambitious Roman governor would take. Throughout his accounts, Luke stressed the impartiality of Roman law. Now he wanted to show how the same law propelled Paul to Rome. ■

MESSAGE
—for—
TODAY

TRYING TO CONVINCE someone of the merits of a religion by rational arguments can prove fruitless. The story of a personal religious experience, however, will often command interest and respect. People may disagree with the interpretation, but they cannot reject the experience. Paul did not argue for his opinions. Instead, he told of his encounter with Jesus on the road to Damascus, and of how he had been chosen by Jesus to preach to those whom he had been persecuting.

When talking about our religious convictions, if we can say, as did the blind man whom Jesus cured, "All I know is that I was blind and now I see [John 9:25]", people will take note – especially if, as in Paul's case, there is an evident change in the way we conduct our lives.

In the EYE of the STORM

The DEPARTURE for ROME
ACTS 27:1–26

" 'So we sailed under the lee of Crete…and struggled along the coast until we came to a place called Fair Havens.' "
ACTS 27:7–8

P AUL AND A NUMBER of other prisoners to be taken to Rome were entrusted to the care of Julius, a centurion. Among the prisoners was Aristarchus, who had accompanied Paul on previous journeys (Acts 20:4), and he may have travelled all the way to Rome (Philemon 24). Luke may also have been with Paul, since the story is told in the first person plural (pp. 34–35).

The group took a ship to Myra, where they changed vessels for an Egyptian grain ship bound for Rome from Alexandria. Struggling against the winds, the new ship made for the sheltered side of Crete and the bay of Fair Havens. Although they were behind schedule, Paul warned them not to proceed farther, because they faced stormy weather as the winter months approached. But Julius, the captain, and the vessel's owner decided to continue to the Cretan harbour of Phoenix nonetheless. They had weighed anchor and set sail, hugging the shore, when they were caught by a hurricane and the crew had to surrender the ship's course to the force of the gale.

They were blown into the lee of an islet off Crete. There, they threw the cargo overboard to lighten the ship and used the ship's boat to undergird, or steady, it. Clouds had obscured the "sun and the stars" – essential aids to ancient

The boat in this Roman mosaic from the AD second to fourth centuries is like the one the crew used to steady the ship and in which they later tried to escape (pp. 82–85).

navigators, who did not have the compass and sextant used to plot courses. Battered by the winds and cast adrift on tumultuous waves, Luke records, "We gave up all hope of surviving." But Paul told them that the previous night, an angel had assured him he was "destined to appear before Caesar" and that God would protect their lives. Paul urged them to have courage and said, "things will turn out just as I was told". They would, however, be stranded on an island.

† Paul: a man of destiny †

Paul was imperilled by natural elements during his voyage to Rome. Luke describes the journey with great relish, and some scholars believe that he may have been influenced by dramatic tales of sea voyages that were fashionable at the time. Few scholars doubt that his account was based on an actual voyage, since the details – the ports, winds, distances and naval terms – are too accurate to suggest otherwise. Still, some think that Luke may have inserted Paul's speeches into a narrative based on another person's voyage. Other scholars, however, believe that the wealth of detail could be due simply to the fact that Luke was a passenger aboard Paul's ship.

Some commentators also think that Luke depicts Paul as a larger-than-life hero; they find it implausible that Paul would have had the chance to dispense nautical advice in the way described. But Paul was a seasoned seafarer. In 2 Corinthians, a letter written before this voyage, Paul said "three times I have been shipwrecked [11:25]". Storms would not have been new to him.

Paul was a compassionate man; this is clear in Acts. He would have found it inconceivable not to warn of bad weather and sailing conditions and to raise morale at a time of crisis. He was also a man of destiny. Christ told him in a vision that he would reach Rome, and an angel confirmed this. In was in Paul's nature to reassure his companions that the worst that would befall them would be to be washed up "on some island". ∎

MESSAGE
—for—
TODAY

PEOPLE OF FAITH are sometimes dismissed as unworldly or unknowing. It is not surprising that the centurion preferred the advice of the ship's captain and of its owner to that given by Paul. But Paul had the direct guidance of God (Acts 27:23), and although he was a captive, he had a compassionate nature – Paul was interested in the well-being of all those aboard the ship.

In this century, too, some of the most influential and practical people, such as Mahatma Gandhi, Mother Teresa of Calcutta, Martin Luther King, Jr., and Archbishop Desmond Tutu, have been people of faith. If our life is based on faith in God, we should, like Paul, be calm and courageous in times of physical danger or emotional crisis. After committing all our actions to God's will, we should be confident that God's care will not fail us.

SHIPWRECKED!

ARRIVING *at* MALTA
ACTS 27:27–28:10

" Paul said to the centurion and his men, 'Unless those men stay on board you cannot hope to be saved.' "
ACTS 27:30–31

AFTER LEAVING the safety of Fair Havens Bay and being cast adrift off Crete, Paul and his companions were at the mercy of gale-force winds for two weeks. But their situation changed "when about midnight the crew sensed that land of some sort was near". The sailors took soundings to measure the depth of the water and found that it was so shallow that they were in danger of running aground, perhaps on a reef. They let down four anchors from the stern to keep the ship steady and prayed for daylight, when they could determine a way to approach the land.

Some of the crew decided to escape in the ship's boat and lowered it on the pretext of laying anchors out from the bow, which involved rowing out a short way. Knowing that it was imperative for everyone's safety that no one leave, Paul warned Julius, the centurion, who had the boat cut away from the ship before the sailors left.

Just before dawn, realising that they all needed every ounce of their strength and energy to reach land, Paul encouraged everyone to eat some food. He himself "took some bread, gave thanks to God in view of them all, broke it, and began to eat", suggesting to some scholars the Eucharistic meal celebrating Jesus' last supper. They all responded to Paul's proposal that everyone eat, and after taking their fill, they threw all the remaining stocks of wheat overboard to lighten the ship.

As the sun rose, they sighted the bay and beach of a land they did not know and prepared to run the ship ashore. They let the anchors slip off their ropes, loosened the ropes of the oars used to steer, hoisted the foresail at the front and headed for land. But before they could reach their goal, their boat hit a shoal, or sandbar: "The bows were wedged in and stuck fast", while rolling waves began to break up the stern.

Fearing that the prisoners would jump ship and swim to their freedom, the contingent of soldiers readied themselves to kill them all. Julius, though, was intent on bringing Paul to Rome and would not consider such an action. Instead, he ordered people who could swim to make for shore and the rest to follow by using planks and bits of flotsam to help them keep afloat. "In this way," Luke says, "it happened that all came safe and sound to land."

✝ Meeting the Maltese ✝

The shipwrecked voyagers soon discovered that they had landed on the island of Malta. The local inhabitants took pity on the drenched, exhausted party and lit a bonfire to warm them. Paul helped to gather brushwood for the fire. But as he was placing it on the fire's flames, a viper appeared from the bundle and "fastened itself on his hand". The superstitious Maltese interpreted this as a sign that Paul was a murderer and that, despite his escape from the sea, "divine justice would not let him live". But Paul shook the snake into the fire and showed no sign of being harmed.

Paul escaping from the shipwreck off Malta is the subject
of this 17th-century Dutch roundel. It is part of a window
in Addington Church, Buckinghamshire.

Taken aback that he had survived the viper, the Maltese now decided that Paul, far from being a murderer, must in fact be a god.

> ❝ *They made us all welcome by lighting a huge fire because…the weather was cold.* ❞
>
> ACTS 28:2

Luke then relates another incident on Malta. Paul was staying with the Roman governor of the island, Publius, whose father was suffering from fever and dysentery. Paul went to see him and, through prayer and the laying on of hands, healed him. News of the cure quickly spread, and Paul found himself healing other sick people. In gratitude, the Maltese honoured Paul and his companions, and when the time came for them to set sail, they provided food for the rest of the voyage.

✝ The hospitable "barbarians" ✝

Luke's story of the shipwreck continues to convey the sense of divine protection surrounding Paul and, by extension, his fellow voyagers to Rome. The details suggest that Luke based his story on an eyewitness account, probably his own. Some scholars, however, question whether the ship could have been large enough to hold the 276 people Luke claims were travelling on it (Acts 27:37); they think the number might be a scribal error for 76. Alexandrian grain ships were known to be large, though, and the Jewish historian Josephus, who was also shipwrecked in this area, wrote that there were 600 people on his vessel, of whom only 80 survived.

Paul and his group were more fortunate: they reached land without loss of life and found the Maltese people welcoming. Although they were of Phoenician stock, Luke refers to them as "barbarians," the neutral Greek term for people who did not speak Greek and were thought to utter strange "bar-bar" sounds. Luke was struck by

The bay in Malta, *where Paul is believed to have been shipwrecked, is now named St. Paul's Bay after him. It is located about 13 km (8 miles) northwest of the modern city of Valletta.*

The vipers *in Malta were poisonous, which is why the Maltese people thought Paul would die when he was bitten. The lively viper shown here is part of a Roman mosaic in the amphitheatre at Badajoz, Spain.*

their "unusual kindness" and by their superstition. In a reversal of the situation at Lystra (pp. 26–29), where the pagan townspeople first thought Paul a god and then pelted him with stones, the Maltese regarded him first as a murderer and then as a god.

Luke states that Paul healed the father of Publius and other sick people who came to him to be cured. The reference to the Maltese honouring "us with many marks of respect" has caused some scholars to speculate whether Luke, by trade a doctor, was called upon to use his medical skills.

Luke ends the episode abruptly. There is no mention of a church being founded or of conversions. This may be because Paul tried to teach the Gospel and failed or because Luke thought it more important to stress Paul's trip to Rome. Regardless, the incidents show the power of God working through Paul. They mirror the signs Jesus linked with true believers: "They will pick up snakes in their hands…they will lay their hands on the sick, who will recover [Mark 16:18]." ∎

MESSAGE
— for —
TODAY

BREAKING BREAD *and giving thanks to God when under threat of being shipwrecked may seem a strange action. Yet Paul did so to affirm that God's power and care was greater than human expectations of disaster. The breaking of bread with thanks has often been celebrated in moments of crisis as well as of joy. Paul urged the church at Thessalonica, "for all things give thanks; this is the will of God [1 Thessalonians 5:18]".*

Giving thanks and remembering God's mercies in the past can inspire confidence and courage for the future. Paul, in his prayers, may have remembered Psalm 107: those caught in a storm at sea prayed to the Lord and, when they were rescued, gave thanks to God for his "faithful love". If we remember to give thanks at all times, we will be more aware that we are surrounded by God's faithful love.

The FINAL ACT

PAUL MEETS *his* DESTINY *in* ROME
ACTS 28:11–31

And so we came to Rome. When the brothers there heard about us they came to meet us, as far as the Forum of Appius and the Three Taverns.

ACTS 28:15

FOR THREE MONTHS, Paul and his party stayed on Malta, waiting for the winter to end before resuming their trip to Rome. They left on another Alexandrian grain ship. Luke mentions that its figurehead was "the Twins" – the Greek gods Castor and Pollux, the protectors of sailors.

Their voyage to Rome took them first to Syracuse in Sicily, then to Rhegium on the toe of Italy. They reached the Bay of Naples and docked at Puteoli (present-day Pozzuoli), which at this time was the most important port in Italy and the terminal for grain ships from Egypt. There, Paul stayed a week with local members of the church.

Heading north by foot on the Via Appia, they came to two stopping places much used by travellers: the Forum of Appius, described by the Roman poet Horace as being full of "stingy tavern keepers", and the Three Taverns. They were 69 and 53 km (43 and 33 miles) from the capital. At both places, Christian brethren from Rome who had heard of Paul's arrival in Italy – presumably from disciples in Puteoli – came to welcome them. "When Paul saw them," Luke says, "he thanked God and took courage."

After they reached the metropolis itself, Paul was "allowed to stay in lodgings of his own" with a soldier to guard him; in other words, he was under house arrest. Once Paul had settled in, he sent a message to the leaders of the Jewish community, requesting that they meet him. They accepted his invitation, and when they arrived, Paul set out his Jewish credentials and told them about his arrest in Jerusalem, his examination by Felix and Festus, and his decision to appeal to Caesar. He tried to convince them that his trial in Jerusalem had hinged on the issue of the "hope of Israel". He was referring to the Jewish hope that the Messiah would come to inaugurate the kingdom of God, a role Paul believed Jesus had fulfilled. It was Paul's intention to show that his imprisonment resulted from his being a loyal Jew.

✝ Paul preaches in Rome ✝

The Jews replied that they had heard nothing about Paul from their brethren in Jerusalem and agreed to see him again to hear his message in more detail. When the day came, a large number of Jews visited Paul. Referring to the scriptures, he tried to persuade them "from early morning until evening" that Jesus was the Messiah. Some of them believed him, but others were sceptical, and the two sides began to argue.

Eventually, as the Jews started to leave, Paul delivered one last message. He told them how accurate the Holy Spirit had been when, speaking through the prophet Isaiah, he had declared that

A.D.G.et in grat. mem. Herberti Mortimer Luckock S.T.P.

hujus Ecclesiae Cathedralis per XVII annos Decani

obd. in Dno. XXIVᵒ die Martii A.S. MCMIX: cujus anⁱ ppitietur Deus

the Jews had cut themselves off from God's word (Isaiah 6:9–10). That was why, Paul said, the Gentiles would receive and listen to the "salvation of God". It was a rebuke Paul had given before during his missions. Yet, in his writings, he demonstrated that he did not consider the Jews to be rejected. In fact, he believed that in time "all Israel will be saved [Romans 11:26]".

Luke ends the Book of Acts by saying that Paul spent the next two years in his lodgings,

Paul is shown bound in chains in this stained-glass window in Lichfield Cathedral, Staffordshire. Although he did not have absolute freedom while in Rome, Paul was allowed to continue preaching.

probably supporting himself through the gifts of the local church or by plying his trade – a practice known to have occurred among Roman prisoners awaiting trial. Although his movements were restricted, Paul continued his work of spreading and strengthening the faith. Many scholars believe that he wrote some of the so-called Captivity Letters (Philippians, Philemon, Colossians and Ephesians) during this period. Also, throughout this period, Paul received many visitors to whom he proclaimed the Gospel "with complete fear-lessness and without any hindrance from anyone".

✝ Paul's ultimate fate ✝

Luke's depiction of Paul's arrival and house arrest in Rome and his missionary work con-ducted from his lodgings represents the climax of Acts. Before, the Gospel had been taken from Judea to the towns and cities of the empire. Now it had reached the very heart of what the Roman writer Pliny the Elder called "a city exceeding in size any other in the world".

As he had done throughout his ministry, Paul first offered the Gospel to the Jews, and only

Remains at the Roman forum include the Temple of Vesta (left), the Arch of Titus (centre), and the Temple of Castor and Pollux, "the Twins" (right).

when it was rejected by them did he turn to the Gentiles. For two years, Paul continued his mis-sionary work from home. What happened to him after this period has been the subject of much speculation. Luke may not have known Paul's ultimate fate at the time he was writing Acts – a view that would conflict with the strong tradition that the book was written after Paul's death.

> 66 *He put his case to them, testifying to the kingdom of God and trying to persuade them...* 99
>
> ACTS 28:23

Some scholars believe that Paul may have been tried and acquitted or that the case against him simply lapsed and that he was freed. Indeed, the Pastoral Letters (1 and 2 Timothy and Titus) seem to refer to a period of Paul's life after Rome. Most scholars, however, believe that these letters were not written by Paul but penned after his death and ascribed to him by their Christian authors, who wanted to uphold Paul's teachings.

The Via Appia in Rome is still in use today. Paul and his companions travelled by foot along this route on their way to Rome.

Another possibility is that Luke knew of Paul's execution (in any event, scholars are united in believing that this was how he died) but preferred to finish on a positive note: the preaching of the Gospel. In support of this, there are references in Acts (for example, 20:23–25) that seem to hint at Paul's martyrdom. On the other hand, if Luke did know that Paul had died at the hands of the Romans, that would seem to be at odds with his favourable portrayal of them throughout the book.

Whatever did happen to Paul, Luke makes it clear that his primary literary concern was the progress of the word of God. In the first chapter of Acts, Luke reports Jesus' predicting that the Gospel would be taken "throughout Judea and Samaria, and indeed to the Earth's remotest end [1:8]". All through Acts, Luke shows how Paul and his companions fulfilled this. He ends his book with Paul preaching openly, without hindrance, in the greatest city of the Western world. His story, in other words, ends in triumph. ∎

MESSAGE
— for —
TODAY

IT MAY BE SURPRISING that Luke's book of Acts does not end with the martyrdom of Paul. It must be remembered, however, that the hero of the story is not a person but God, and the theme centres on the Gospel and how it reached Rome. The climax of Acts is Paul's "proclaiming the kingdom of God" in Rome, the centre of the known world at that time. This fulfilled the words of the Risen Christ (Acts 1:8).

Today, some people feel that the church is failing. Yet many others see abundant evidence that God is still in control and that God's spirit continues to empower the spread of the Gospel. Only a small fraction of the population of Rome would have visited Paul, but it was enough to ensure that, in time, the good news of salvation was proclaimed throughout Europe and across the world.

ABOUT *the* CITIES VISITED

OF THE MANY PLACES Paul stopped at on his journeys, there are some still in existence, although sometimes known by a different name. Yet many others have long since disappeared.

ANTIOCH (PISIDIA) ACTS 13:14–51; 14:21
Located in the province of Galatia, Antioch in Pisidia held a strong position on the slopes of a mountain. In Paul's time, Romans, Greeks, Phrygians and Jews lived in this important city. Only ruins remain, by the Turkish town of Yalvaç.

ANTIOCH (SYRIA) ACTS 13:1–4; 14:26–15:2; 15:30–34; 18:22
The third largest city in the Roman Empire, Antioch was the capital of Syria. It was built along the Orontes River, which flows into the Mediterranean Sea. It was an early centre of Christianity, and the name "Christian" was coined there.

ATHENS ACTS 17:16–33
Ancient Greece's greatest city-state, Athens was built around the Acropolis, or hill. The Romans spread the culture and teachings of the Athenians throughout the Roman Empire after conquering the city. Today, Athens is the capital of modern Greece, and its ancient buildings, such as the Parthenon, draw tourists from around the world.

CAESAREA ACTS 20:1–16
The capital of the Roman province Judea, Caesarea had impressive civic buildings – a legacy of King Herod the Great (37–34 BC) – and some of them have been excavated. Its magnificent port was destroyed by Muslims in the 13th century. A kibbutz was founded near the site in 1940.

CORINTH ACTS 18:1–17
With two harbours and a major land route passing through it, Corinth was conveniently placed to prosper from trade. The Romans destroyed it in

146 BC. Julius Caesar rebuilt the city in 46 BC and repopulated it with freed slaves and the poor. Today, Corinth is an export centre for Greece.

EPHESUS ACTS 19:1–20:1
A free city in the Roman province of Asia, at its peak Ephesus was the largest trading port. By Paul's time, it was in decline because its harbour was silting up. Now the city's ruins, including the almost intact theatre where the riot took place, lie near Seljuq, in the Turkish province of Izmir.

ICONIUM ACTS 14:1–5
First settled by Phrygian people, Iconium prospered under the Romans. Its wealth was derived from agriculture and trade, and the city, which stood at the intersection of five roads, was a centre of communications. Now known as Konya, it is the capital of the largest province in Turkey.

JERUSALEM ACTS 21:17–23:32
Since King David's time, Jerusalem has been the spiritual centre of Jewish life. Jews in all parts of the world face the city to pray. In 63 BC, Roman procurators replaced the Jewish rulers of Jerusalem, leading to revolts and the near destruction of the city. The Romans destroyed the city in AD 70 but later rebuilt it. Today, Jerusalem is a spiritual centre for the Jewish, Christian and Muslim faiths and is regarded as the capital of Israel.

LYSTRA ACTS 14:6–20
Lystra was a small Roman colony – a town where Roman soldiers settled for retirement – established in 6 BC. Little of Lystra remains in Turkey.

MALTA ACTS 27:27–28:10
A Mediterranean island, Malta came under Roman rule in 218 BC. As part of the Roman Empire, it was governed by a proconsul in Paul's time. Today it is an independent island.

MILETUS Acts 20:15–38

Miletus thrived as the capital of Ionia until it was destroyed by the Persians in 494 BC. By Paul's time, the city had been rebuilt but its harbours had silted up, and the city was in decline. Ruins still remain near the modern city of Söke in Turkey.

PHILIPPI Acts 16:11–40

A Roman colony on the Egnatian Way, Philippi was named after Philip II of Macedon (359–336 BC). Its few remains lie near Kavalla, Greece.

ROME Acts 28:14–31

The city of Rome was the heart of the Roman Empire. Augustus Caesar rebuilt it in New Testament times, claiming to have found "the city built of brick" and "left it built of marble". Today, Rome is the centre of the Catholic church and the capital of Italy. It holds several Pauline sites, such as St. Paul's Outside-the-Walls Church.

THESSALONICA Acts 17:1–15

In 42 BC the Romans granted Thessalonica permission to to be a self-governed city. It is now the industrial city Thessaloniki in Greece, second in population only to Athens.

TYRE Acts 21:3–15

The principal town of Phoenicia, a region of Syria, Tyre was built on an island joined to the mainland by an artificial causeway. The town is now known as Sur and is located in Lebanon.

BIBLIOGRAPHY

Alexander, D., Alexander, P. (eds.) *The Lion Handbook to the Bible* Lion Publishing, Berkhamstead, 1973

Anderson, Bernard W. *The Living World of the Old Testament* Longman, London, 1978

Barclay, William *The Acts of the Apostles* St. Andrews Press, Edinburgh, 1973
– *The Mind of Saint Paul* Fontana, London, 1965

Barraclough, Geoffrey (ed.) *The Times Atlas of World History* HarperCollins, London, 1993

Dodd, C.K. *The Meaning of Paul* Fontana, London, 1978

Frank, Harry Thomas *Discovering the Biblical World* Hodder and Stoughton, Ohio, 1975

Gardner, Joseph L. (ed.) *Atlas of the Bible* Reader's Digest, New York, 1981

Gower, Ralph *The New Manners and Customs of Bible Times* Moody Press, Chicago, 1987

Hanson, R.P.C. *The Acts* Oxford University Press, Oxford, 1967

Hunter, A.M. *The Gospel According to Paul* SCM Press, London, 1966

Jewett, Robert *Dating Paul's Life* SCM Press, London, 1979

Keller, Werner *The Bible as History* BCA, London, 1974

Larkin Jr., William J. *Acts* Inter-Varsity Press, Illinois, 1995

Maccoby, Hyam *Paul and Hellenism* SCM Press, London, 1991

Marshall, I. Howard *The Acts of the Apostles* William B. Eerdmans Publishing Company, Grand Rapids, Michigan/Inter-Varsity Press, Leicester, UK, 1980

May, Herbert G. *Oxford Bible Atlas* Oxford University Press, Oxford, 1974

Meinardus, Otto F.A. *St. Paul in Greece* Lycabettus Press, Athens, 1992

Pax, Wolfgang E. *In the Footsteps of St. Paul* Leon Amiel, New York, 1977

Richards, Lawrence O. (ed.) *The Applied Bible Dictionary* Kingsway Publications, Eastbourne, England, 1990

Rogerson, John *The New Atlas of the Bible* Macdonald & Co. (Publishers) Ltd., London, 1985

Sanders, E.P. *Paul and Palestinian Judaism* SCM Press, London, 1977
– *Paul* Oxford University Press, Oxford, 1991

Sherwin-White, Adrian N. *Roman Society and Roman Law in the New Testament* Oxford University Press, Oxford, 1963

Stendahl, K. *Paul Among Jews and Gentiles* Fortress Press, Philadelphia, 1976

Theissen, Gerd *The Social Setting of Pauline Christianity* Fortress Press, Philadelphia, 1982

INDEX

Page numbers in **bold** denote main mentions; numbers in *italics* refer to illustrations and their captions; *mp* and *M* indicate maps and the Message for Today box, respectively.

F

Fair Havens, in Crete 70*mp*, 80, 82
Felix, procurator of Judea 71, 74, **76**, 79
Festus, Porcius, procurator of Judea 71, **76–79**, *77–78*
fortune-teller, of Philippi 36
Forum of Appius 70*mp*, 86

G

Gaius, in Ephesus 57
Galatia 14–15*mp*, 30*mp*, 32, **34**, 52*mp*, 53, 54, 70*mp*
Galilee, early church 13
Gallio, proconsul of Achaea 48–51, *50*
Gamaliel, Rabbi 7
Gandhi, Mahatma 81*M*
Gentiles 15, 18, 20, 21, **23**
and circumcision **31**, 32
Jews and 8, 13, 23, 25
God-fearers **20**, 23, **25**, 40, 44, 48
pagans **26–29**, **44–47**, 54–59, *55–56*
Greece 30*mp*, 32, 35, **44–51**, 53, 60
see also Macedonia; Achaea

H

healing
by Paul 26, *27*, 55, **56–57**, *57*, 58, 61, 84, 85
by Philip 66
Hellenists 10
Hermes 26, 28
Herod I the Great 75
Herod Agrippa *see* Agrippa II
Horace 86

I

Iconium 14–15*mp*, 15, 22, *24*, **24–25**, 26, 30*mp*, 34, 52*mp*, **90**, 91*mp*
Illyricum 30*mp*, 52*mp*, 53
Italy 70*mp*, 86

J

James, brother of Jesus 31, 72
Jason, of Thessalonica 40, 43
Jerusalem 30*mp*, 52–53*mp*, 63, 65, 66, 71*mp*, **90**, 91*mp*
Antonia Fortress 72, *74*
Christians persecuted 15, 66
church council **31**, 32
famine 16, 67
Paul arrested in *see under* Paul
Paul collects money for 16, 53, 57, 60, 76
Paul in 7, 10, 13, 16, 51, 53, 67–69, 70*mp*, 72
synagogue *41*
Temple 74
Jews
Diaspora 25
exorcists 56
Law, and Gentile Christians 31
Law, and intermarriage 34
Nazirite vow 72, 74
opposed to Christians **10**, 15, 24–25, 26, 28, **40**, **42–43**, 48–50, *50, 54–55*, 63
Paul accused by 71, **72–79**
synagogue *41*
John the Baptist 54
John Mark 16–20, *22*, 32–33
travels with Barnabas 31, 32, **33**
Judaism *see* Jews
Judas, of Damascus 10
Judas Barsabbas, of Jerusalem 31
Judea 13, 30*mp*, 53*mp*, **66–69**, 71*mp*
Julius, centurion 80, 82
Justus, of Corinth 48, 50

K

Karakus Mountains *22*
King, Martin Luther 81*M*

L

Last Supper *60*, 61, 82
Lesbos 52*mp*, 62
Lewis, C.S. 13*M*

L (cont.)

Lucius of Cyrene 16
Luke **8**, 85
Acts written by 7, **8–9**, 88–89
in Macedonia 34
travels with Paul 8, **35**, 60, 62, 66, 68, 80–81
see also Acts
Lycaonia 14–15*mp*, 26
Lycia 52*mp*, 66, 70*mp*
Lydia, of Philippi 36, 38, 39, *39*
Lysias, Claudius, tribune 75, 76
Lystra 14–15*mp*, 15, **26–28**, 30*mp*, 32, 33–34, 46–47, 52*mp*, 85, **90**, 91*mp*

M

Macedonia 30*mp*, 32, 34–35, **36–43**, 48, 52*mp*, 53, 57, 60, 70*mp*
Maeander River *65*
Malta 70*mp*, **82–86**, *83–85*, **90**, 91*mp*
Manaen, of Antioch 16
Mark *see* John Mark
Messiah/Christ 15, **20**, 23, 25, **41**, **43**, 48, 86
Miletus 52*mp*, **62–5**, *64–65*, 66, 68, **91**, 91*mp*
Myra 70*mp*, 80
Mysia 30*mp*, 32, 34

N

Nazarene sect 76
Neapolis 30*mp*, 36, *42*, 52*mp*
Nero, Emperor 8, 50, **71**

O

Ovid 28
oxen 26, *29*

P

pagans *see under* Gentiles
Palestine, early church 13
Palmyra *68*
Pamphylia 14–15*mp*, 20, 29, 52–53*mp*, 70–71*mp*

ACKNOWLEDGMENTS

ILLUSTRATION
David Atkinson (maps); Debbie Hinks (illustration symbols).

PICTURE CREDITS
t = top, b = bottom
1 AKG London; 2–3 Sonia Halliday Photogaphs; 3 Ancient Art & Architecture Collection; 5 Laura Lushington/Sonia Halliday Photographs; 6 Ancient Art & Architecture Collection; 9 Bodleian Library, Oxford/AKG London; 11 Bibliotheque Nationale, Paris/Bridgeman Art Library; 12 F.H.C. Birch/Sonia Halliday Photographs; 13 Sonia Halliday Photographs; 17 Bridgeman Art Library; 18 Sonia Halliday Photographs; 19 Erich Lessing/AKG London; 21 Victoria & Albert Museum/Erich Lessing/AKG London; 22–24 Sonia Halliday Photographs; 27 Laura Lushington/Sonia Halliday Photographs; 28–29 Sonia Halliday Photographs; 33 Bodleian Library, Oxford/AKG London; 34 Sonia Halliday Photographs; 35 Jane Taylor/Sonia Halliday Photogaphs; 37 Laura Lushington/Sonia Halliday Photographs; 38 Sonia Halliday Photographs; 39 James Carmichael/NHPA; 41 Robert Harding Picture Library; 42t Sonia Halliday Photographs; 42b F.H.C. Birch/Sonia Halliday Photographs; 45 Victoria & Albert Museum/ Bridgeman Art Library; 46 F.H.C. Birch/Sonia Halliday Photographs; 49 Cecil Higgins Art Gallery, Bedford/Bridgeman Art Library; 50 AKG London; 51 Sonia Halliday Photographs; 55 Giraudon/Bridgeman Art Library; 56 Sonia Halliday Photographs; 57 AKG London; 58 Ancient Art & Architecture Collection; 58-60 E.T. Archive; 63 Ancient Art & Architecture Collection; 64 E.T. Archive; 65-67 Sonia Halliday Photographs; 68t Jane Taylor/ Sonia Halliday Photographs; 68b Erich Lessing/ AKG London; 73 Ancient Art & Architecture Collection; 74 Jane Taylor/Sonia Halliday Photographs; 75 E.T. Archive; 77 Laura Lushington/ Sonia Halliday Photographs; 78t E.T. Archive; 78b Erich Lessing/ AKG London; 80 Ancient Art & Architecture Collection; 83 Laura Lushington/Sonia Halliday Photographs; 84 Index/ Bridgeman Art Library; 84-85 T.C. Rising/Sonia Halliday Photographs; 87 Laura Lushington/Sonia Halliday Photographs; 88 Sonia Halliday Photographs; 89 Paul Milner/Sonia Halliday Photographs; 96 Ancient Art & Architecture Collection.

If the publisher has unwittingly infringed copyright in any of the illustrations reproduced, they would pay an appropriate fee on being satisfied of the owner's title.

The burial of Paul is illustrated in this 13th-century Italian fresco. The cause of Paul's death remains a mystery, but some scholars believe that he was executed in Rome.